try Cross-Stitch

try Cross-Stitch

try Cross-Stitch

try Cross-Stitch

try Cross-Stitch

try Cross-Stitch

try Cross-Stitch

try Cross-Stitch

8-Color Country Cross-Stitch

8-Color Country Cross-Stitch

Sarah Stevenson

A STERLING/CHAPELLE BOOK
Sterling Publishing Co. Inc.   New York

For Chapelle Limited

Owner: Jo Packham

Staff: Sandra Anderson, Trice Boerens, Malissa Boatwright, Rebecca Christensen, Holly Fuller, Sharon Ganske, Cherie Hanson, Holly Hollingsworth, Susan Jorgensen, Susan Laws, Amanda McPeck, Tammy Perkins, Jamie Pierce, Leslie Ridenour, Nancy Whitley, and Lorrie Young

Designers: Trice Boerens, Polly Carbonari, Jamie Pierce, and Mike Vickery

Photographer: Kevin Dilley for Hazen Photography

All photographs featured in this book were taken at the home of Jo Packham.

Library of Congress Cataloging-in-Publication Data

Stevenson, Sarah
        Eight color country cross-stitch / by Sarah Stevenson.
            p.   cm.
        "A Sterling/Chapelle Book."
        Includes index.
        ISBN 0-8069-1288-X
        1. Cross-stitch--Patterns. I. Title.
TT778.C76S73 1995
746.44'3021--dc20   94-46330
                                                                            CIP

10 9 8 7 6 5 4 3 2 1

A Sterling/Chapelle Book

Published by Sterling Publishing Company, Inc.
387 Park Avenue South, New York, N.Y. 10016
© 1995 by Chapelle Ltd.
Distributed in Canada by Sterling Publishing
c/o Canadian Manda Group, One Atlantic Avenue, Suite 105
Toronto, Ontario, Canada M6K 3E7
Distributed in Great Britain and Europe by Cassell PLC
Wellington House, 125 Strand, London WC2R 0BB, England
Distributed in Australia by Capricorn Link (Australia) Pty Ltd.
P.O. Box 6651, Baulkham Hills, Business Center, NSW 2153, Australia
Printed and Bound in Hong Kong
All Rights Reserved

ISBN 0-8069-1288-X

Welcome to Eight-Color Country Cross-Stitch!

Contents

Chapter One
Friendly Country Hello

Country Home   10
American Antiques   11
Hunter's Rest   16
Angler's Rest   17
Country Garden   22
Christmas Sleigh   23

Chapter Two
Clear Country Morning

Home Sweet Home   34
Come On In   35
Bunnies in a Basket   38
"C" Is for Cat   39
Espresso Yourself   44
Three Coffee Cups   45
Farm Fresh   50
Sunshine House   51

Chapter Three
A Country Quilting Bee

Country Farm   58
Goose Waddle   59
Fence Rails   64
Hen and Chicks   65
Cats in the Corner   70
Christmas Star   71

Chapter Four
Angelic Country Charm

Heavenly Tea	78
Baby's Guardian Angel	79
Gardening Angel	86
Wedding Angel	87
Cowgirl Angel	94
Native American Angel	95
Earth Angel	102
Summer Celebration Angel	104
The Heart Is Always Young	105
Give Away Love	110
Be Loveable	111
Fun and Easy Decoupage Frames	115

Chapter Five
Country Holiday Cheer

Peaceable Kingdom Sampler and Ornaments	118
Peaceable Kingdom Stocking	119
And They Came With Haste…	128
Noel Stocking	132
Season's Greetings	133
General Instructions	142
Metric Equivalency Chart	143
Index	143

Friendly Coun

Friendly Coun

Friendly Coun

Friendly Coun

Friendly Coun

Friendly Coun

Friendly Coun

try Hello

try Hello

try Hello

try Hello

try Hello

try Hello

try Hello

Chapter One

Country Home

Country Home

Stitched on pewter Murano 30 over 2 threads, the finished design size is 5⅝" x 7½". The fabric was cut 12" x 14". For alphabet, see page 29.

Fabrics — Design Size

Fabrics	Design Size
Aida 11	7⅝" x 10⅛"
Aida 14	6" x 8"
Aida 18	4⅝" x 6¼"
Hardanger 22	3⅞" x 5⅛"

Anchor		DMC (used for sample)	

Step 1: Cross-stitch (2 strands)

Anchor		DMC	
1	·		White
24	□	776	Pink-med.
117	△	341	Blue Violet-lt.
130	○	799	Delft-med.
185	–	964	Seagreen-lt.
210	✕	562	Jade-med.
942	╱	738	Tan-vy. lt.
401	●	844	Beaver Gray-ultra dk.

Step 2: Backstitch (1 strand)

401	⌐	844	Beaver Gray-ultra dk.

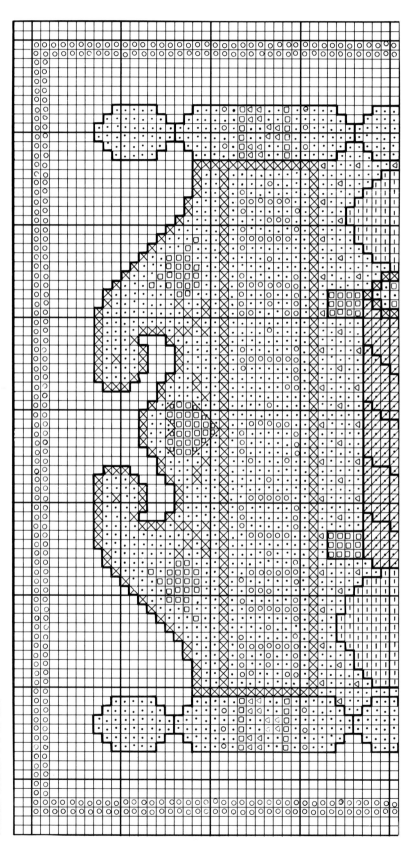

Stitch Count: 84 x 112

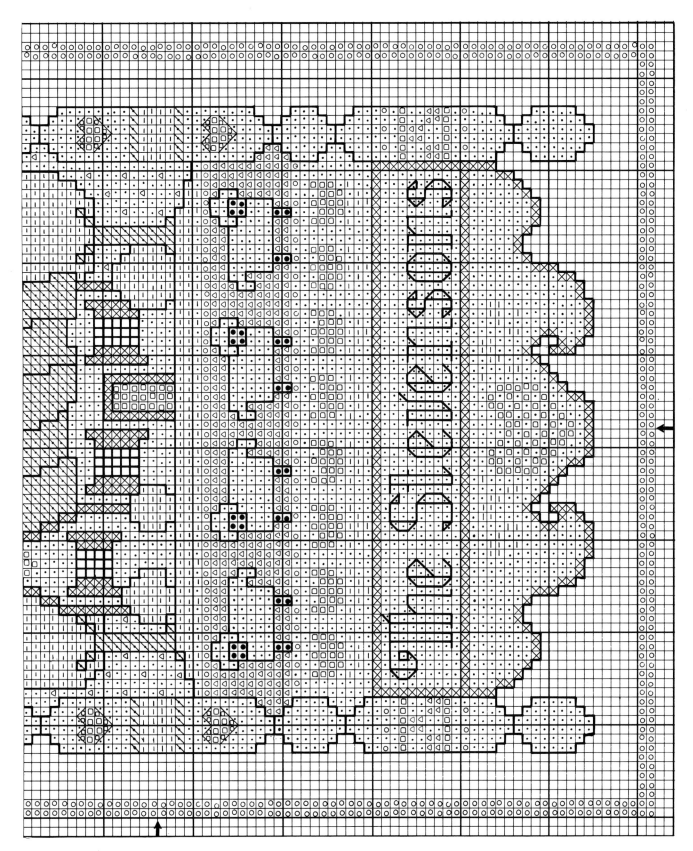

American Antiques

Stitched on oatmeal Floba 25 over 2 threads, the finished design size is 6¾" x 9". The fabric was cut 13" x 15" framed. For alphabet, see page 29.

Fabrics   Design Size
Aida 11   7⅝" x 10⅛"
Aida 14   6⅝" x 7¼"
Aida 18   4⅝" x 6¼"
Hardanger 22   3⅞" x 5⅛"

Anchor			DMC	(used for sample)
			Step 1: Cross-stitch (2 strands)	
387			712	Cream
891			676	Old Gold-lt.
101			327	Antique Violet-vy. dk.
121			793	Cornflower Blue-med.
267			470	Avocado Green-lt.
309			781	Topaz-dk.
349			301	Mahogany-med.
403			310	Black

Step 2: Backstitch (1 strand)

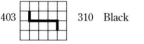

403		310	Black

Step 3: French Knot (1 strand)

403		310	Black

Stitch Count: 84 x 112

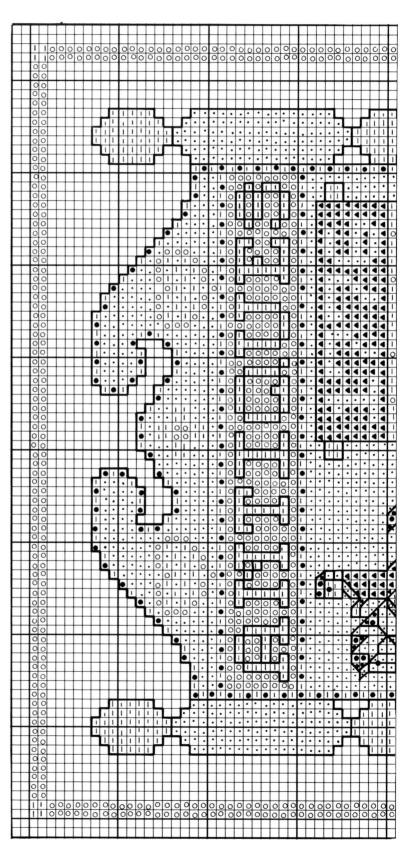

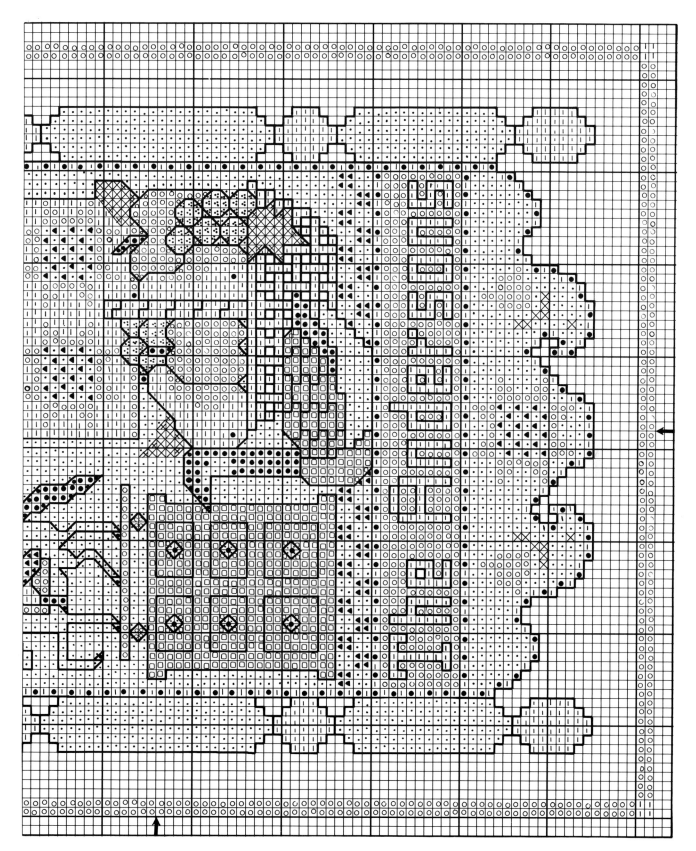

Hunter's Rest

Hunter's Rest

Stitched on light mocha Cashel linen 28 over 2 threads, the finished design size is 5" x 7". The fabric was cut 11" x 13". For alphabet, see page 30.

Fabrics	Design Size
Aida 11	6⅜" x 8⅞"
Aida 14	5" x 7"
Aida 18	3⅞" x 5⅛"
Hardanger 22	3⅛" x 4½"

Anchor				DMC (used for sample)	
Step 1: Cross-stitch (2 strands)					
1					White
187				958	Seagreen-dk.
888				371	Mustard
246				895	Christmas Green-dk.
885				739	Tan-ultra vy. lt.
363				436	Tan
349				301	Mahogany-med.
403				310	Black

Step 2: Backstitch (1 strand)

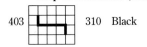

| 403 | 310 | Black |

Country Welcome Banners

To turn your warm country welcome signs into the banners you see in the photos, just follow the quick and easy directions below.

Materials

Finished design trimmed to 7½" x 10"
7¾" x 10" fabric for backing
   (for fringed banner, use Aida)
Matching thread
Hanging rod (twig, cinnamon stick, dowel, etc.)

Directions

1. Lay design and fabric backing right sides together. Stitch along sides and bottom. Turn and press. Whipstitch top closed.

2. For fringed banner, lay designed Aida and blank Aida wrong sides together 1" from inside edge. Sew a small zigzag stitch all around piece. Pull out threads along outside to fray.

3. Fold top edge over top of rod and mark with a pin. Remove rod and stitch to form casing. Replace rod and hang as desired.

Angler's Rest

Stitched on rue green Belfast linen 32 over 2 threads, the finished design size is 5¼" x 7". The fabric was cut 12" x 13". For alphabet, see page 30.

Fabrics	Design Size
Aida 11	7⅝" x 10⅛"
Aida 14	6" x 8"
Aida 18	4⅝" x 6¼"
Hardanger 22	3⅞" x 5⅛"

Anchor		DMC (used for sample)

Step 1: Cross-stitch (2 strands)

926	·		Ecru
896	▲	3721	Shell Pink-dk.
161	–	3760	Wedgewood-med.
189	O	991	Aquamarine-dk.

Step 2: Backstitch (1 strand)

236		3799	Pewter Gray-vy. dk.

Stitch Count: 84 x 112

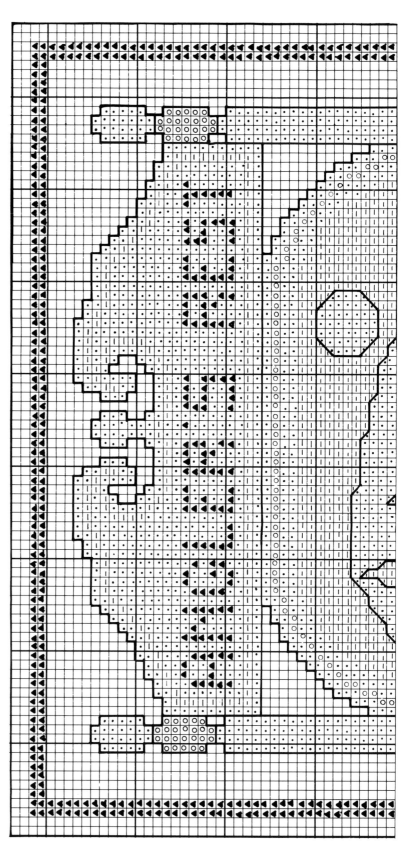

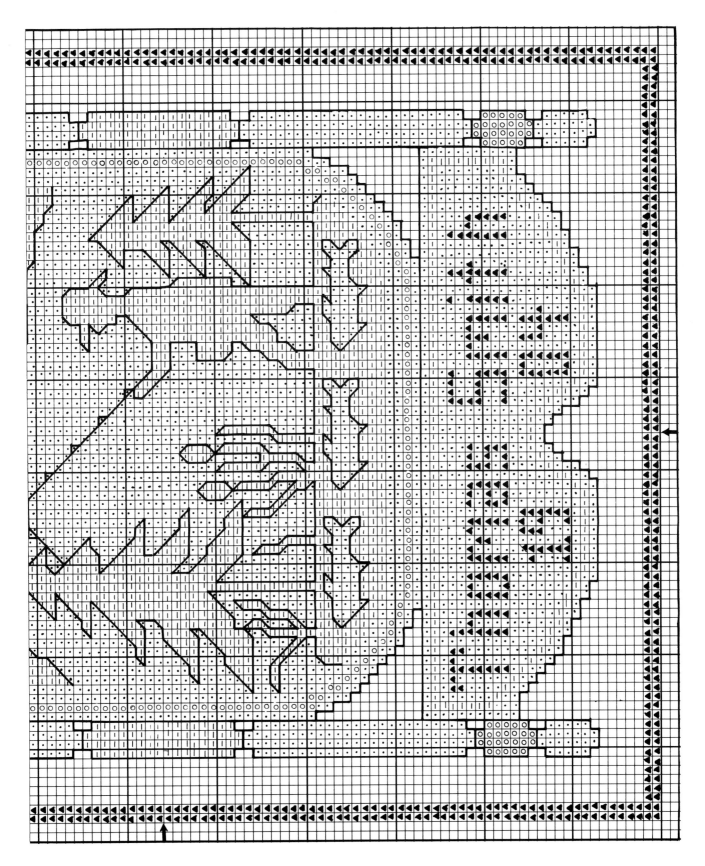

Country Garden

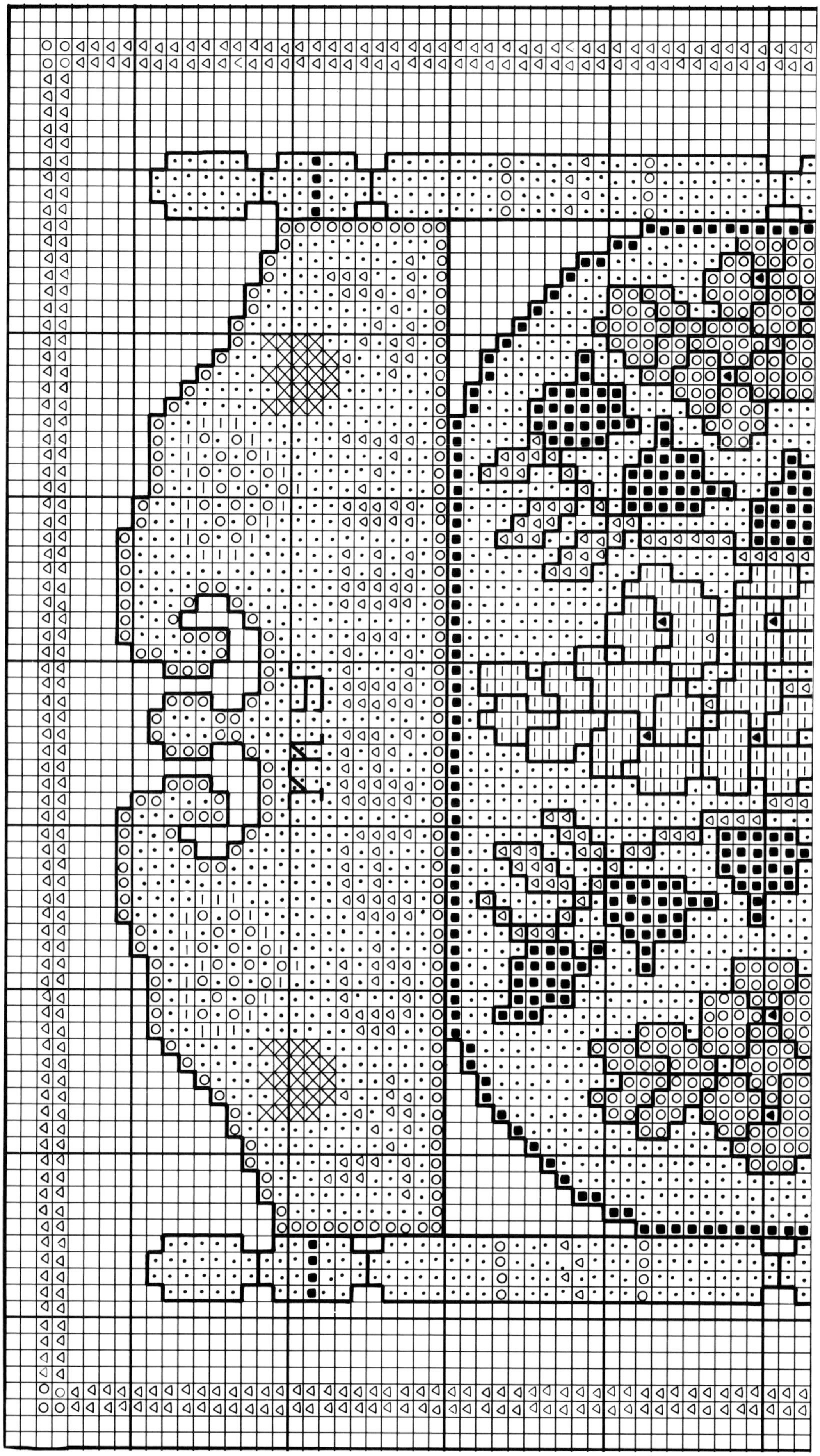

Stitch Count: 84 x 112

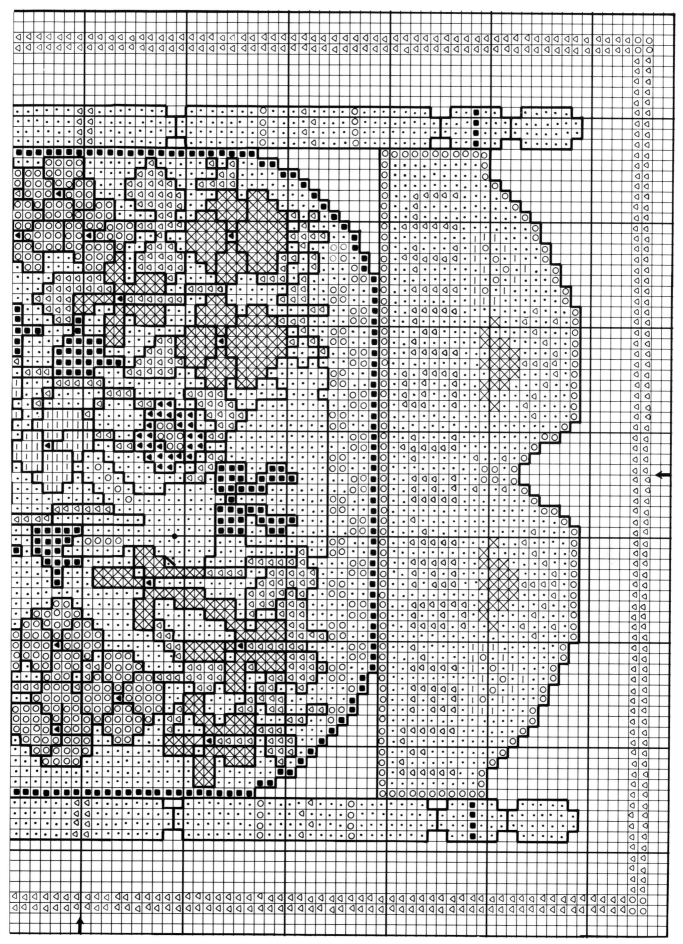

Country Garden

Stitched on ivory Murano 30 over 2 threads, the finished design size is 5⅝" x 7½". The fabric was cut 12" x 14". Graph begins on page 24. For alphabet, see page 31.

Fabrics	Design Size
Aida 11	7⅝" x 10⅛"
Aida 14	6" x 8"
Aida 18	4⅝" x 6¼"
Hardanger 22	3⅞" x 5⅛"

Anchor　　**DMC (used for sample)**

Step 1: Cross-stitch (2 strands)

Anchor		DMC	
1	·		White
293	▲	727	Topaz-vy. lt.
10	–	352	Coral-lt.
75	⊙	3733	Dusty Rose-lt.
159	■	3325	Baby Blue-lt.
118	✕	340	Blue Violet-med.
208	△	563	Jade-lt.

Step 2: Backstitch (1 strand)

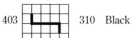

403	310	Black

Step 3: French Knot (1 strand)

403	●	310	Black

Christmas Sleigh

Stitched on ash rose Murano 30 over 2 threads, the finished design size is 5¾" x 8". The fabric was cut 12" x 14". Graph begins on page 27. For alphabet, see page 31.

Fabrics	Design Size
Aida 11	7⅞" x 10⅞"
Aida 14	6⅛" x 8⅝"
Aida 18	4¾" x 6⅝"
Hardanger 22	3⅞" x 5½"

Anchor　　**DMC (used for sample)**

Step 1: Cross-stitch (2 strands)

Anchor			DMC	
1	·	⁄		White
890	▲	⁄	729	Old Gold-med.
10	I	⁄	3712	Salmon-med.
13	⊙	⁄	347	Salmon-vy. dk.
816	–	⁄	3750	Antique Blue-vy. dk.
862	△	⁄	3362	Pine Green-dk.
8581	✕	⁄	3022	Brown Gray-med.
403	●	⁄	310	Black

Step 2: Backstitch (1 strand)

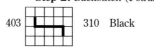

403	310	Black

Step 3: French Knot (1 strand)

403	●	310	Black

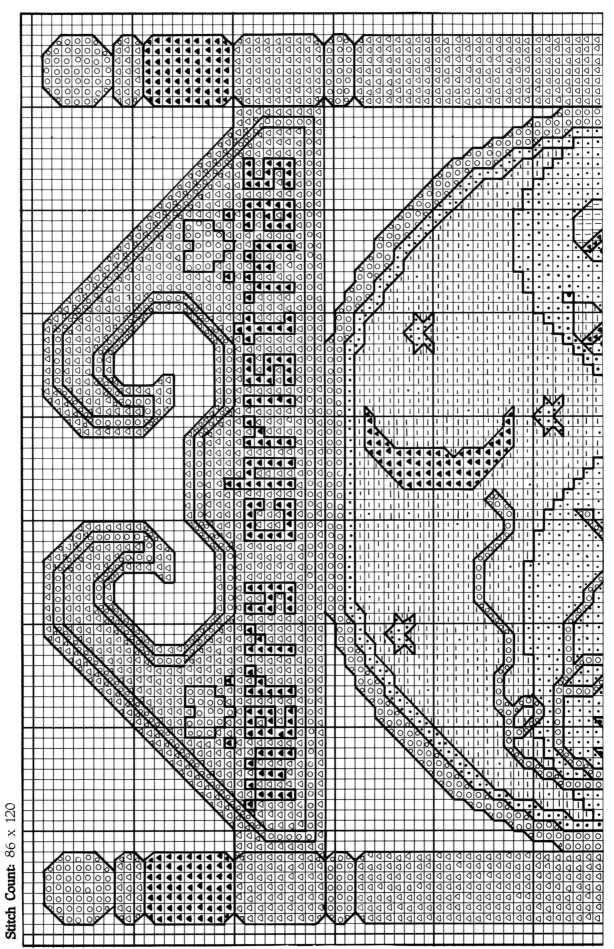

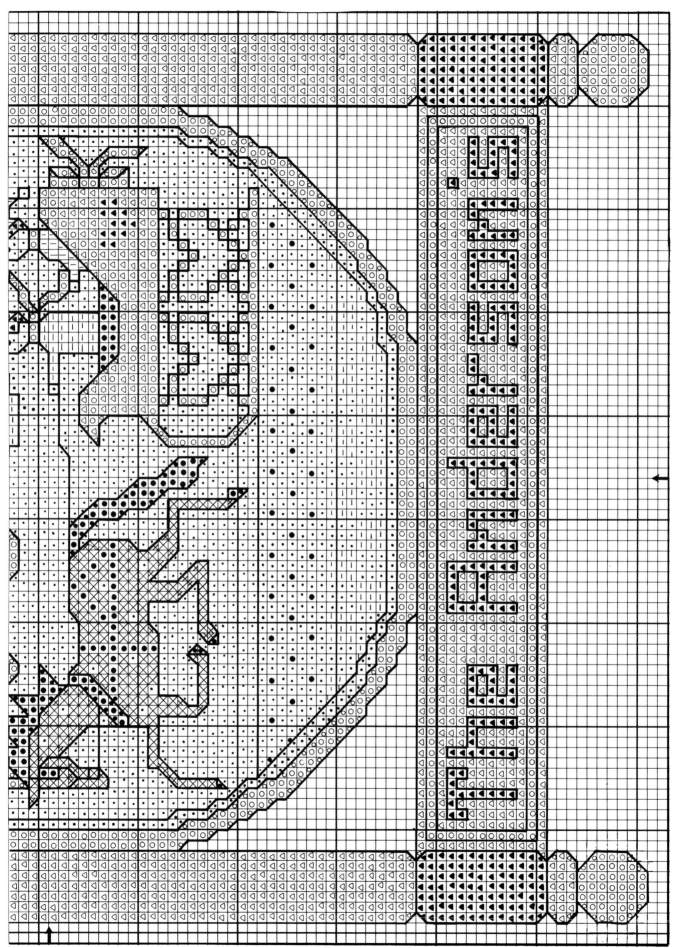

Country Home Alphabet

See page 12.

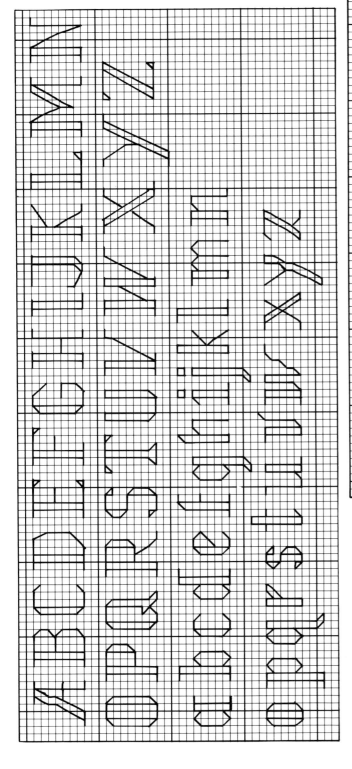

American Antiques
Alphabet

See page 14.

Hunter's Rest Alphabet
See page 19.

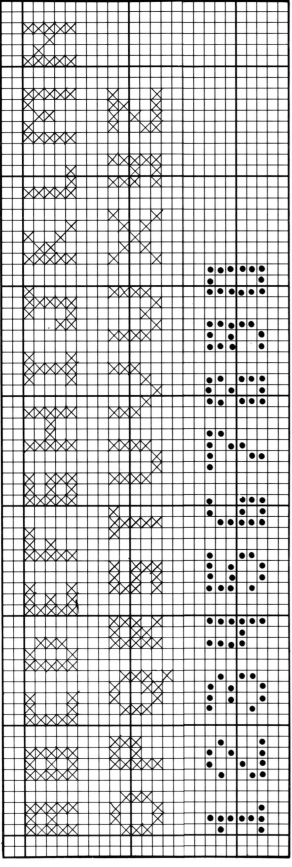

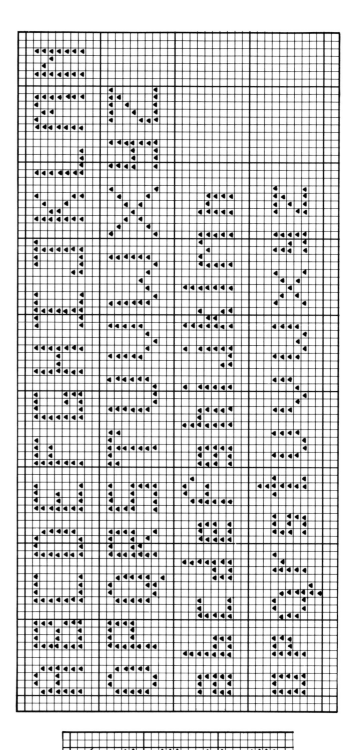

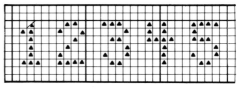

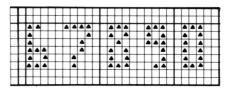

Angler's Rest Alphabet
See page 20.

Country Garden Alphabet
See page 26.

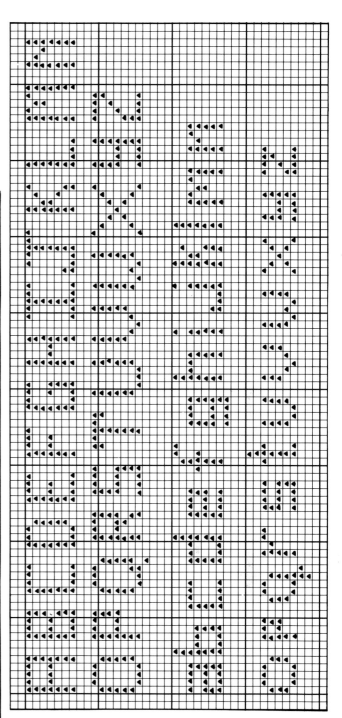

Christmas Sleigh Alphabet
See page 26.

Clear Country

Clear Country

Clear Country

Clear Country

Clear Country

Clear Country

Clear Country

Morning

Morning

Morning

Morning

Morning

Morning

Morning

Chapter Two

Home Sweet Home

Home Sweet Home

Stitched on white Belfast linen 32 over 2 threads, the finished design size is 2¾" x 2¾". The fabric was cut 9" x 9".

Fabrics	Design Size
Aida 11	4" x 4"
Aida 14	3⅛" x 3⅛"
Aida 18	2⅜" x 2⅜"
Hardanger 22	2" x 2"

Stitch Count: 43 x 43

Anchor		DMC (used for sample)	
Step 1: Cross-stitch (2 strands)			
49	·	963	Wild Rose-vy. lt.
22	●	816	Garnet
104	∴	210	Lavender-med.
940	O	792	Cornflower Blue-dk.
203	△	564	Jade-vy. lt.
210	▲	562	Jade-med.
378	–	841	Beige Brown-lt.
380	×	839	Beige Brown-dk.

Step 2: Backstitch (1 strand)

Anchor		DMC	
940		792	Cornflower Blue-dk. (around word home, blue in cup)
210		562	Jade-med. (around word sweet, flowers in back ground)
380		839	Beige Brown-dk. (all else)

Come On In

Stitched on white Belfast linen 32 over 2 threads, the finished design size is 4¼" x 6⅝". The fabric was cut 11" x 16".

Fabrics	Design Size
Aida 11	6⅛" x 9⅝"
Aida 14	4⅞" x 7⅝"
Aida 18	3¾" x 5⅞"
Hardanger 22	3⅛" x 4⅞"

Anchor			DMC (used for sample)	
Step 1: Cross-stitch (2 strands)				
886	·	◿	677	Old Gold-vy. lt.
59	–	◿	326	Rose-vy. dk.
154	O	◿	3755	Baby Blue
167	+		598	Turquoise-lt.
206	I	◿	955	Nile Green-lt.
204	△	◿	912	Emerald Green-lt.
309	∴	◿	435	Brown-vy. lt.
905	☐	◿	3031	Mocha Brown-vy. dk.

Step 2: Backstitch (1 strand)

Anchor		DMC	
905		3031	Mocha Brown-vy. dk.

Bunnies in a Basket

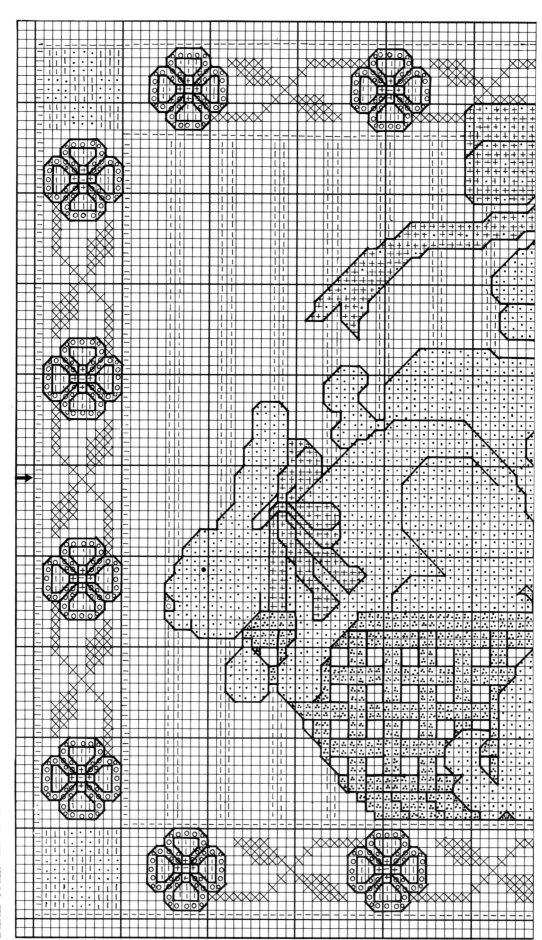

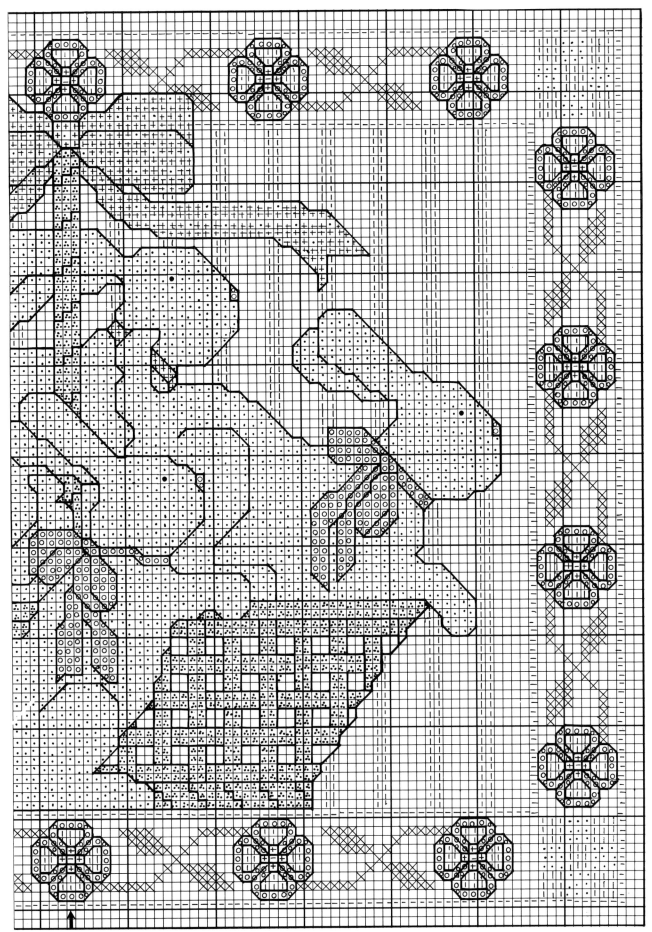

Bunnies in a Basket

Stitched on cream Murano 30 over 2 threads, the finished design size is 8½" x 6½". The fabric was cut 15" x 13". Graph begins on page 40.

Fabrics	Design Size
Aida 11	11½" x 8⅞"
Aida 14	9⅛" x 6⅞"
Aida 18	7" x 5⅜"
Hardanger 22	5¾" x 4⅜"

Anchor		DMC (used for sample)	
Step 1: Cross-stitch (2 strands)			
1			White
886		677	Old Gold-vy. lt.
306		725	Topaz
881		945	Peach Beige
11		3328	Salmon-dk.
203		564	Jade-vy. lt.
210		562	Jade-med.
403		310	Black

Materials

Finished design trimmed to 11" x 9"
¾ yard light green fabric
Matching thread
3¾ yards eyelet lace
Stuffing

Directions

All seams ½".

1. Cut light green fabric in the following sizes: two 3" x 13" strips, two 3" x 11" strips, three 2½" x 45" strips, and one 15" x 13½" piece.

2. Place 11" strips, right sides down, on top and bottom edges of cross-stitch. Sew and press seams open. Place 13" strips, right sides together, on sides of cross-stitch. Sew and press seams open.

3. For ruffle, sew 45" strips together and roll-hem outer edge. Lay on top of lace and run a zigzag basting stitch over strong thread ½" from edge. Gather ruffle by pulling thread. Place ruffle on front of pillow with ruffles pointing in. Adjust gathers around edge and pin into place. Baste ruffle onto pillow.

4. Lay back piece, 15" x 13½", with right side down, on top of pillow. Sew around sides, leaving an opening to turn.

5. Clip corners, turn and stuff firmly. Slipstitch opening closed.

"C" Is for Cat

Stitched on antique white Cashel linen 28 over 2 threads, the finished design size is 5⅝" x 7¼". The fabric was cut 12" x 14". Graph begins on page 43.

Fabrics	Design Size
Aida 11	7⅛" x 9⅛"
Aida 14	5⅝" x 7¼"
Aida 18	4⅜" x 5⅝"
Hardanger 22	3½" x 4⅝"

Anchor		DMC (used for sample)	
Step 1: Cross-stitch (2 strands)			
891		676	Old Gold-lt.
59		326	Rose-vy. dk.
159		827	Blue-vy. lt.
161		826	Blue-med.
246		986	Forest Green-vy. dk.
363		436	Tan
370		434	Brown-lt.
Step 2: Backstitch (1 strand)			
381		938	Coffee Brown-ultra dk.
Step 3: French Knot (1 strand)			
381		938	Coffee Brown-ultra dk.

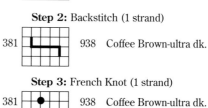

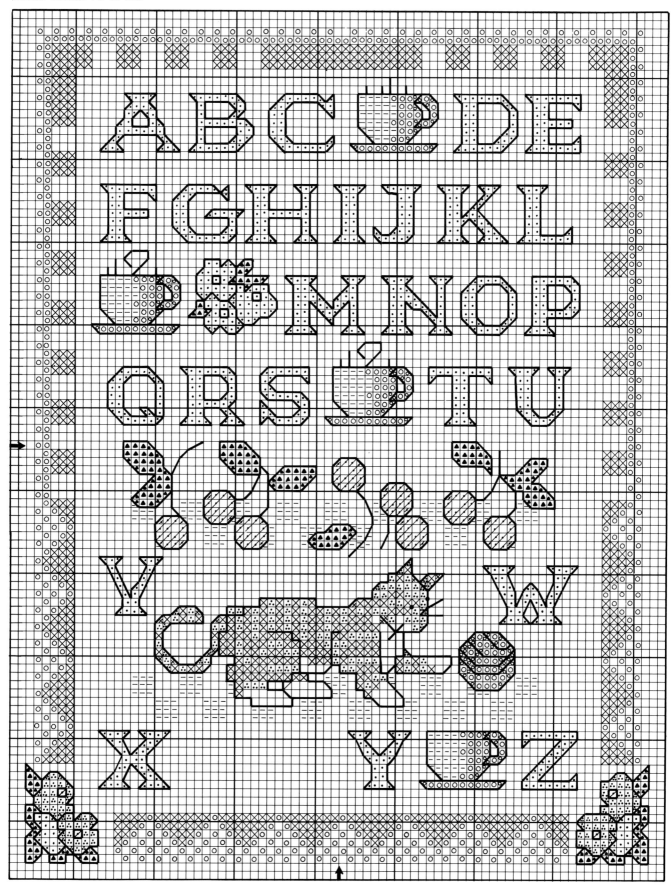

Espresso Yourself

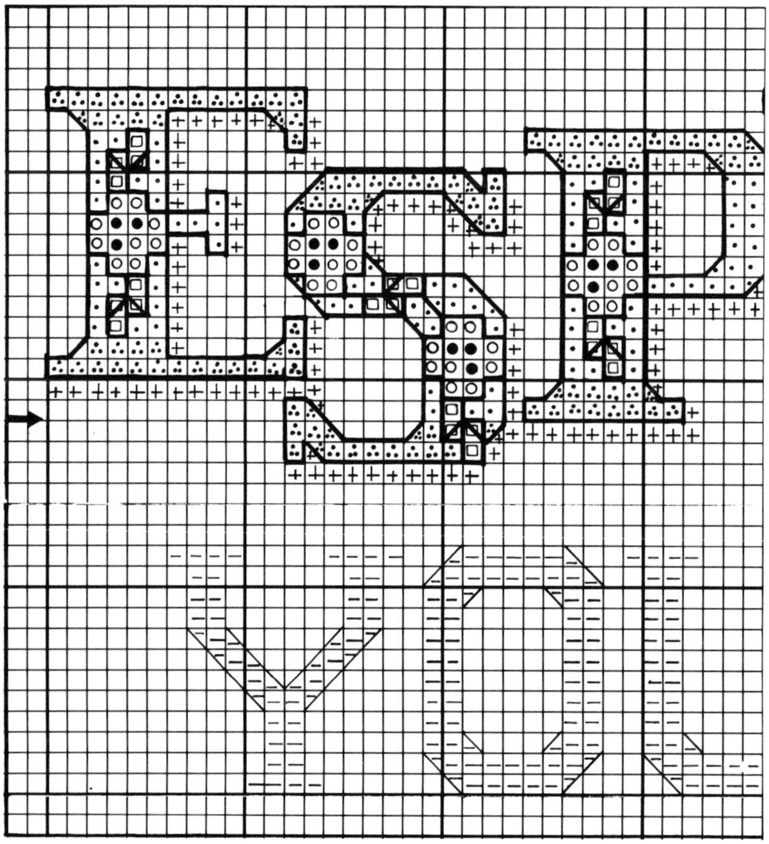

Stitch Count: 100 x 36

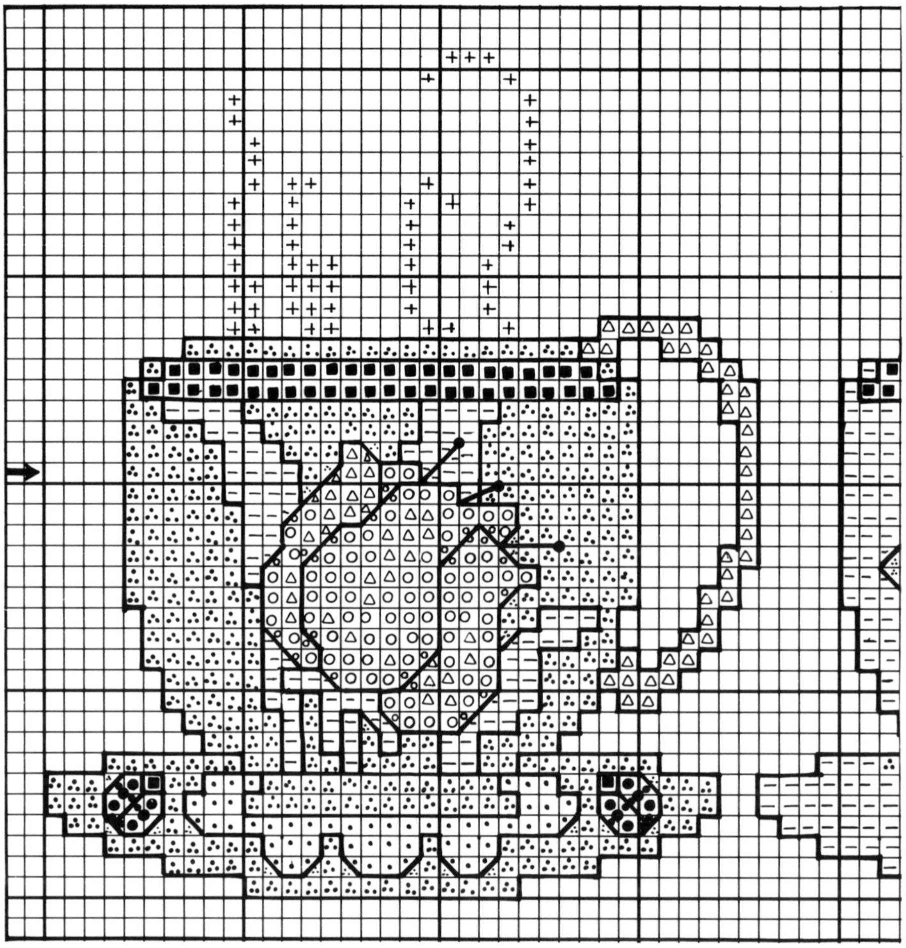

Stitch Count: 108 x 41

Espresso Yourself

Stitched on pewter Murano 30 over 2 threads, the finished design size is 6⅝" x 2⅜". The fabric was cut 13" x 9". Graph begins on top half of page 46.

Fabrics	Design Size
Aida 11	9⅛" x 3¼"
Aida 14	7⅛" x 2⅝"
Aida 18	5½" x 2"
Hardanger 22	4½" x 1⅝"

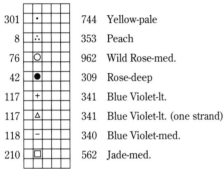

Anchor		DMC (used for sample)	
Step 1: Cross-stitch (2 strands)			
301	·	744	Yellow-pale
8	∴	353	Peach
76	O	962	Wild Rose-med.
42	●	309	Rose-deep
117	+	341	Blue Violet-lt.
117	△	341	Blue Violet-lt. (one strand)
118	–	340	Blue Violet-med.
210	□	562	Jade-med.

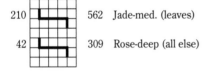

Anchor		DMC (used for sample)	
Step 2: Backstitch (1 strand)			
210		562	Jade-med. (leaves)
42		309	Rose-deep (all else)

Three Coffee Cups

Stitched on antique white Cashel linen 28 over 2 threads, the finished design size is 7¾" x 2⅞". The fabric was cut 17" x 8". Graph begins on bottom half of page 46.

Fabrics	Design Size
Aida 11	9⅞" x 3¾"
Aida 14	7¾" x 2⅞"
Aida 18	6" x 2¼"
Hardanger 22	4⅞" x 1⅞"

Anchor		DMC (used for sample)	
Step 1: Cross-stitch (2 strands)			
300	·	745	Yellow-lt. pale
303	△	742	Tangerine-lt.
9	O	760	Salmon
13	●	347	Salmon-vy. dk.
160	–	813	Blue-lt.
189	∴	991	Aquamarine-dk.
378	+	841	Beige Brown-lt.
380	■	839	Beige Brown-dk.

Anchor		DMC (used for sample)	
Step 2: Backstitch (1 strand)			
380		839	Beige Brown-dk.

Three Coffee Cups
Antique Thread Spool

Materials

5" x 7" antique thread spool
Two 4" circles of mat board
Small tea set painted to match cross-stitch
Finished design cut to 17" x 8"
Matching thread
30" blue cording
6" circle white doily
Cutout doily motifs
1 yard each yellow, pink, and blue silk ribbon
Stuffing
Wood stain
Wood glue

Directions

1. Stain wooden thread spool. Set aside.

2. Remove one end of antique thread spool. Cut holes in center of mat circles according to the diameter of the spool dowel.

3. Fold finished piece in half right sides together to form tube. Sew ¼" seam along short side. Run a gathering stitch along each end of the tube. Gather one end of tube to fit mat circle. Glue one mat circle to inside of gathered end, leaving center hole visible. Slide covered mat circle hole over spool dowel and glue to spool end. Let dry.

4. Stuff tube firmly around spool dowel. Slide remaining mat circle onto spool dowel. Pull gathering thread to cover mat circle with fabric, leaving center hole visible. Glue fabric to mat circle.

5. Replace wood end of antique thread spool and glue with wood glue. Glue cording around top and bottom where fabric meets spool ends.

6. To embellish, glue doily around top of spool. Glue tea set to thread spool. Glue smaller doily motifs to larger doily. Using all three silk ribbons, knot one end to doily, leaving about three inches. Loop silk ribbons around tea set and tie a small bow around teapot. Loop silk ribbons again and knot to doily. Knot ends on ribbon and secure to design with small stitches (see photo).

The finished thread spool can be used as a decorative pin keeper.

Farm Fresh

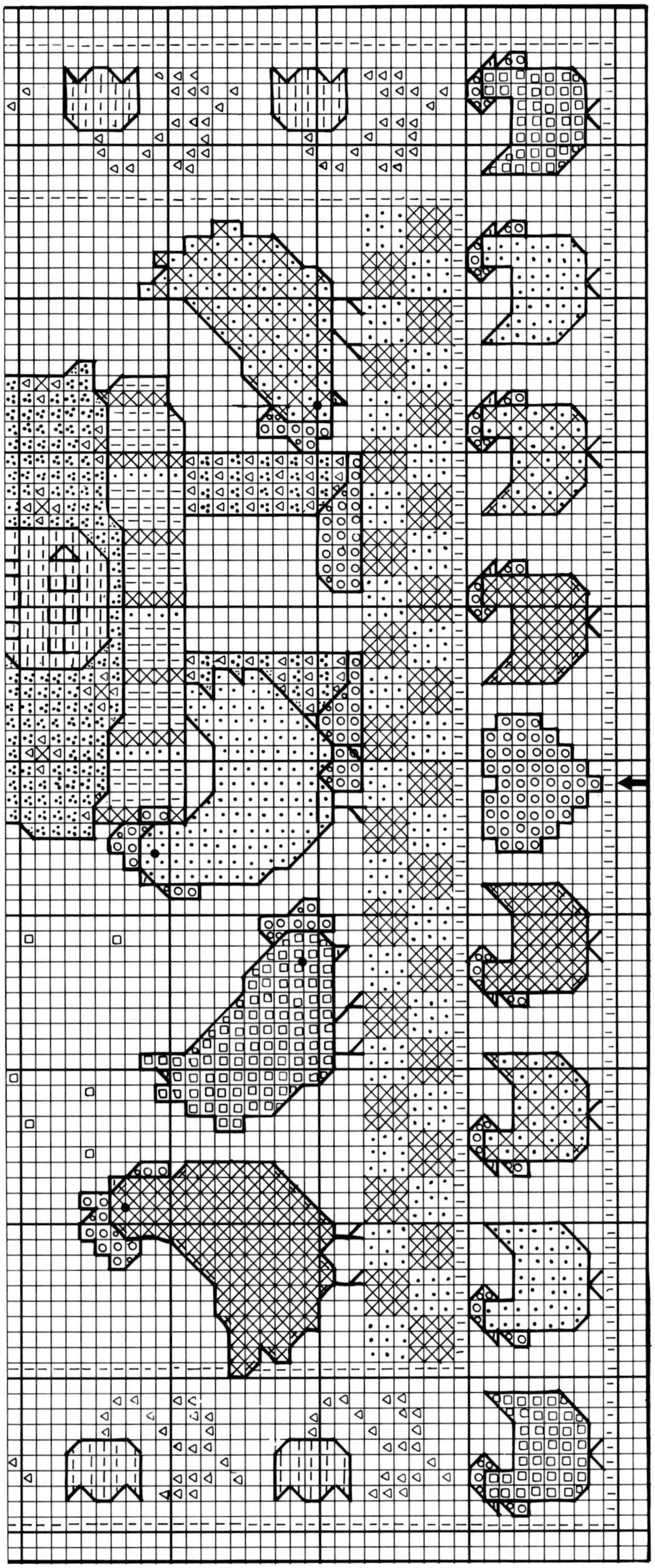

Farm Fresh

Stitched on oatmeal Floba 25 over 2 threads, the finished design size is 7¾" x 9½". The fabric was cut 14" x 16".

Fabrics	Design Size
Aida 11	8⅞" x 10⅞"
Aida 14	6⅞" x 8½"
Aida 18	5⅜" x 6⅝"
Hardanger 22	4⅜" x 5⅜"

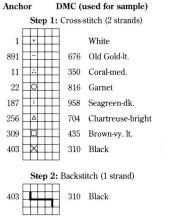

Anchor		DMC (used for sample)	
	Step 1: Cross-stitch (2 strands)		
1	•		White
891	−	676	Old Gold-lt.
11	∴	350	Coral-med.
22	○	816	Garnet
187	ı	958	Seagreen-dk.
256	△	704	Chartreuse-bright
309	□	435	Brown-vy. lt.
403	╳	310	Black
	Step 2: Backstitch (1 strand)		
403	⌐	310	Black

Sunshine House

Stitched on white Murano 30 over 2 threads, the finished design size is 7⅜" x 10½". The fabric was cut 14" x 17". Graph begins on page 54.

Fabrics	Design Size
Aida 11	10" x 14⅜"
Aida 14	7⅞" x 11¼"
Aida 18	6⅛" x 8¾"
Hardanger 22	5" x 7⅛"

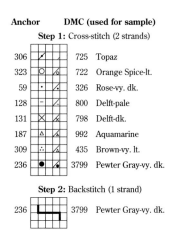

Anchor			DMC (used for sample)	
	Step 1: Cross-stitch (2 strands)			
306	⁄	⁄	725	Topaz
323	○	⁄○	722	Orange Spice-lt.
59	•	⁄•	326	Rose-vy. dk.
128	−	⁄−	800	Delft-pale
131	╳	⁄╳	798	Delft-dk.
187	△	⁄△	992	Aquamarine
309	∴	⁄∴	435	Brown-vy. lt.
236	●	⁄●	3799	Pewter Gray-vy. dk.
	Step 2: Backstitch (1 strand)			
236	⌐		3799	Pewter Gray-vy. dk.

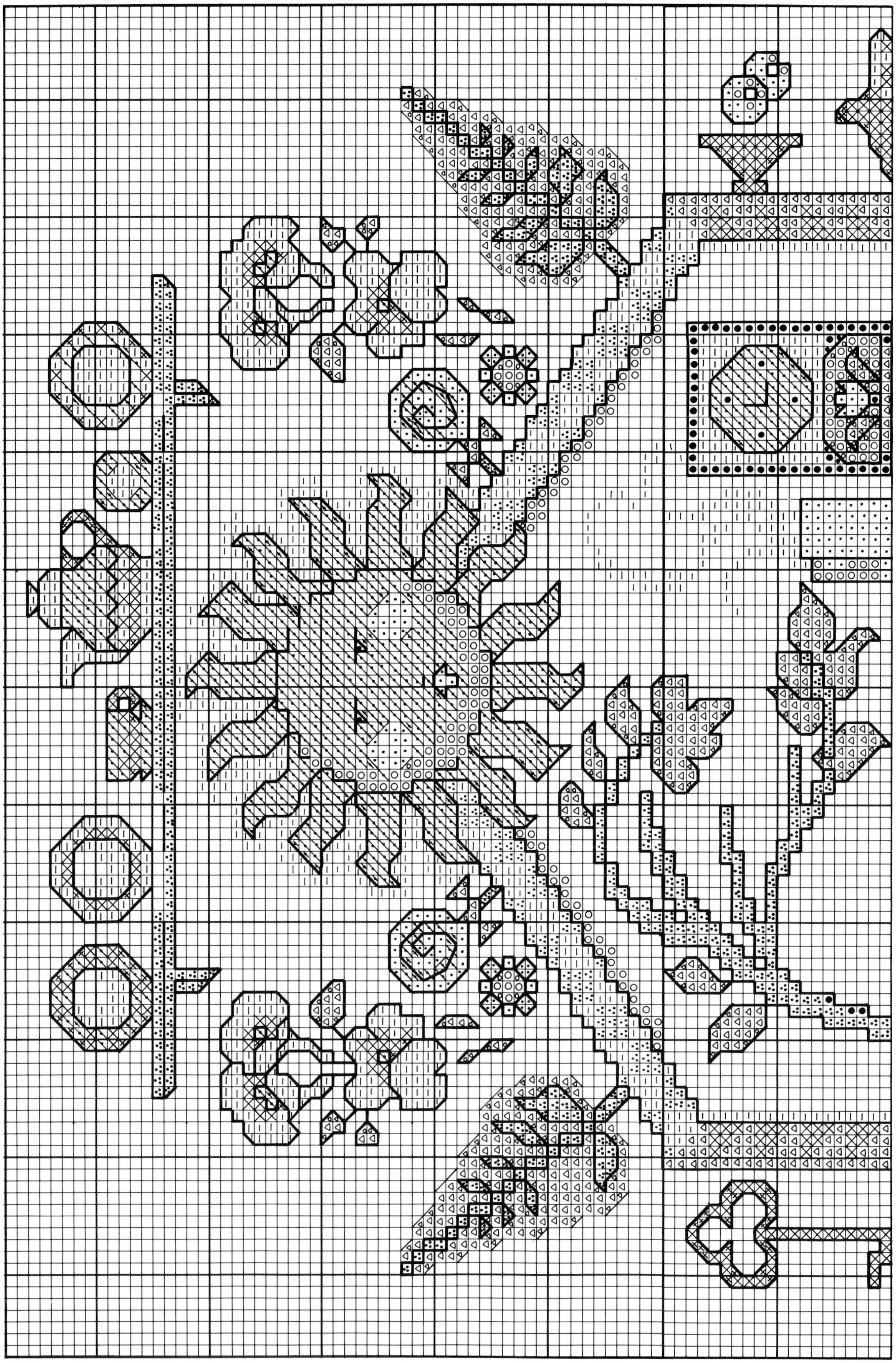

Stitch Count: 111 x 158

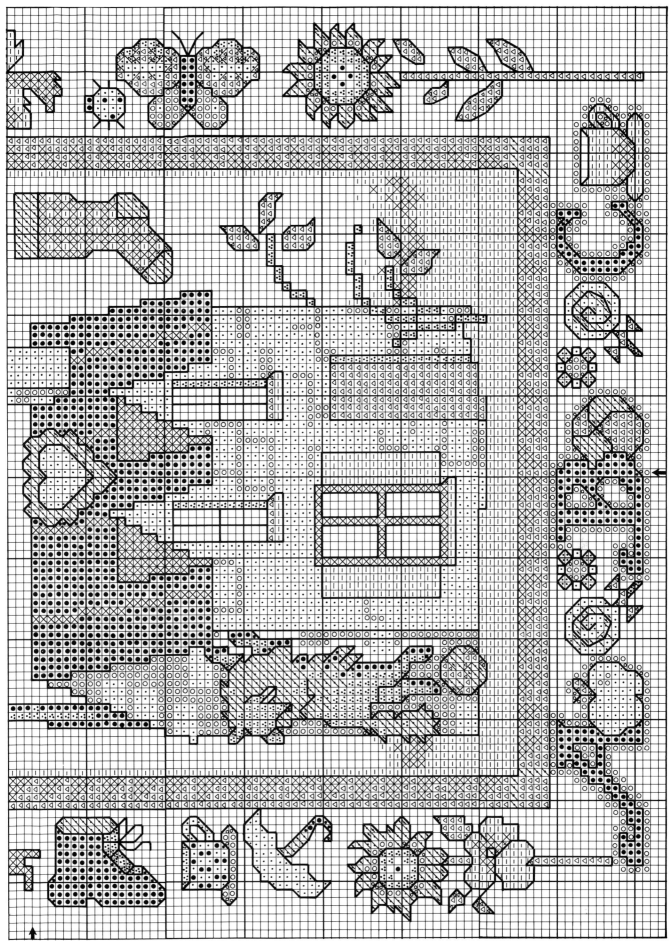

A Country Qu
A Country Qu
A Country Qu
A Country Qu
A Country Qu
A Country Qu
A Country Qu

Quilting Bee

Chapter Three

Country Farm

Goose Waddle

Country Farm

Stitched on cream Murano 30 over 2 threads, the finished design size is 6⅝" x 7½". The fabric was cut 13" x 14".

Fabrics	Design Size
Aida 11	9⅛" x 10⅛"
Aida 14	7⅛" x 8"
Aida 18	5½" x 6¼"
Hardanger 22	4½" x 5⅛"

Anchor		DMC (used for sample)	
Step 1: Cross-stitch (2 strands)			
1	·		White
TBA	X	3820	Dark Straw
9	O	760	Salmon
130	△	799	Delft-med.
214	–	966	Baby Green-med.
5968	∴	355	Terra Cotta-dk.
956	□	613	Drab Brown-lt.
403	●	310	Black
Step 2: Backstitch (1 strand)			
403		310	Black
Step 3: French Knot (1 strand)			
403	●	310	Black

Stitch Count: 100 x 112

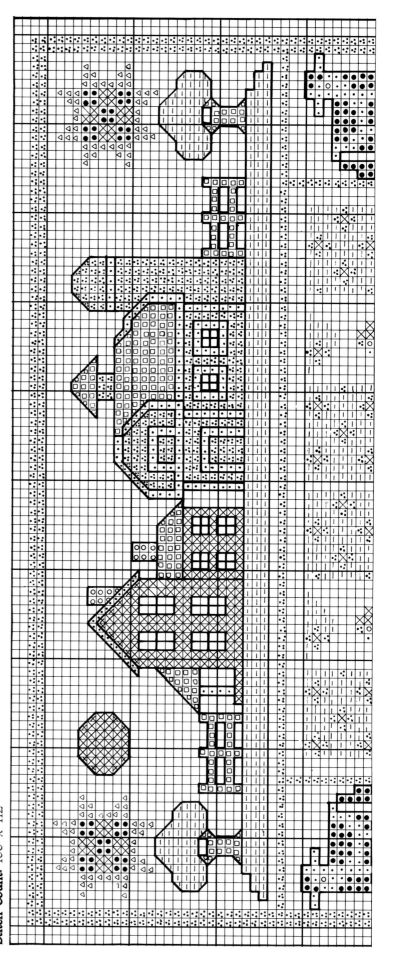

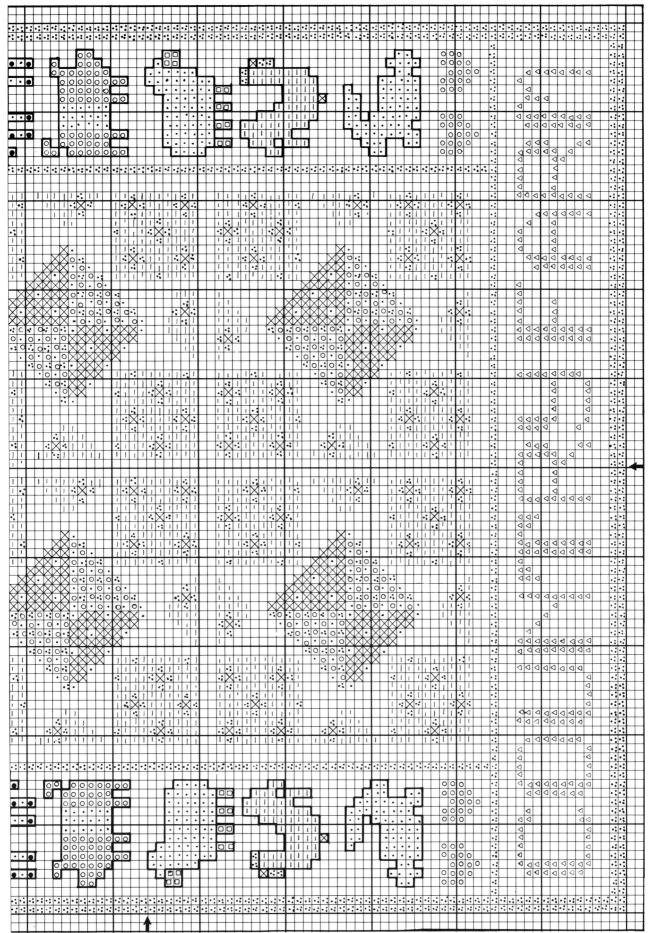

Goose Waddle

Stitched on white Murano 30 over 2 threads, the finished design size is 7¼" x 6⅞". The fabric was cut 14" x 13".

Fabrics
Aida 11
Aida 14
Aida 18
Hardanger 22

Design Size
9⅞" x 9½"
7¾" x 7⅜"
6" x 5¾"
4⅞" x 4¾"

Anchor		DMC (used for sample)	
Step 1: Cross-stitch (2 strands)			
1	·		White
301	X	744	Yellow-pale
8	△	761	Salmon-lt.
159	−	3325	Baby Blue-lt.
185	O	964	Seagreen-lt.
187	∴	958	Seagreen-dk.
347	●	402	Mahogany-vy. lt.
403	▲	310	Black
Step 2: Backstitch (1 strand)			
403	L	310	Black

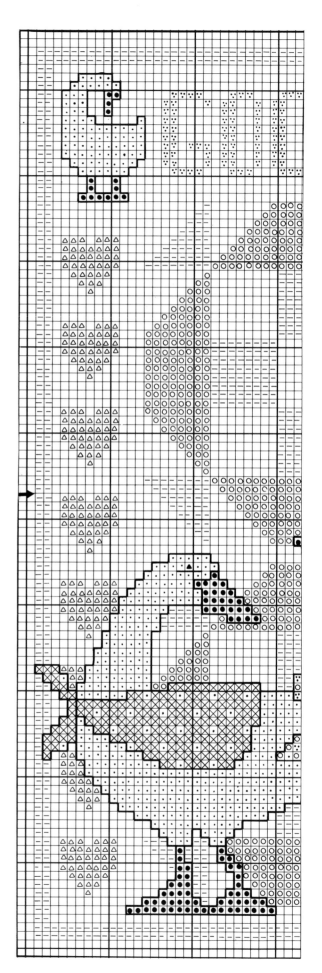

Stitch Count: 108 x 104

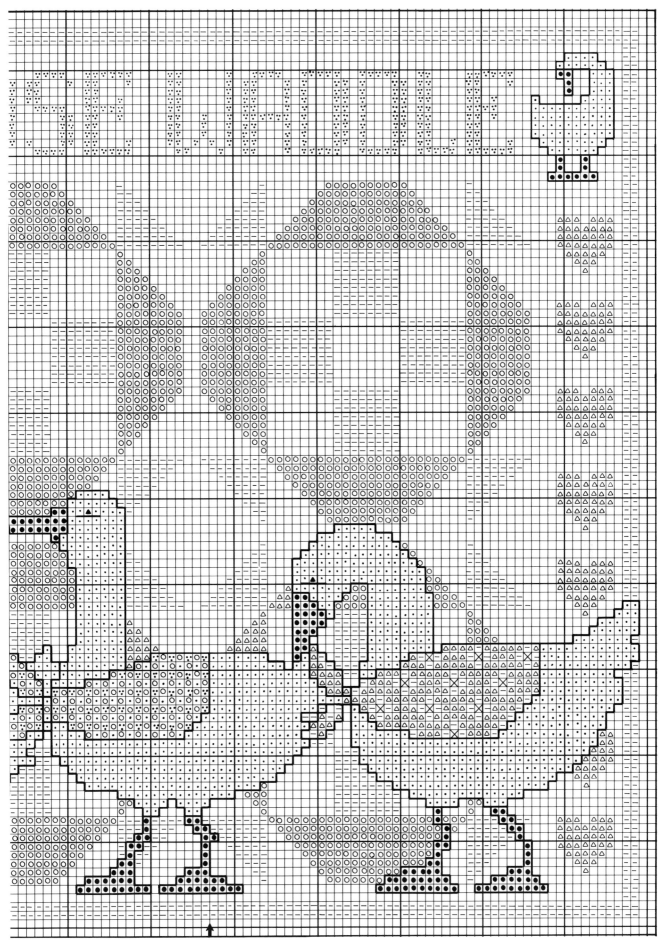

Fence Rails

Hen and Chicks

Fence Rails

Stitched on platinum Belfast linen 32 over 2 threads, the finished design size is 6¾" x 6½". The fabric was cut 13" x 13".

Fabrics	Design Size
Aida 11	9⅞" x 9½"
Aida 14	7¾" x 7⅜"
Aida 18	6" x 5¾"
Hardanger 22	4⅞" x 4¾"

Anchor		DMC (used for sample)

Step 1: Cross-stitch (2 strands)

Anchor	Symbol	DMC	Color
1	ı		White
886	O	677	Old Gold-vy. lt.
892	∴	225	Shell Pink-vy. lt.
158	△	828	Blue-ultra vy. lt.
128	□	800	Delft-pale
214	–	368	Pistachio Green-lt.
899	•	3782	Mocha Brown-lt.
403	X	310	Black

Step 2: Backstitch (1 strand)

403		310	Black

Materials

Finished design trimmed to 7½" square
13" square pastel green fabric
Three 1½" x 36" strips of green, blue, white, and
        pink pastel fabric
Matching thread
13" square quilt batting

Directions

All seams ¼"

1. From each color cut one 8¼" strip, one 10" strip and one 11½" strip.

2. Staring with shortest strips, sew blue strip along bottom edge of design. Continue counter-clockwise with pink, white, and green. Start second row at bottom with white and third row at bottom with pink (see photo).

(Instructions continued on page 68)

Stitch Count: 108 x 104

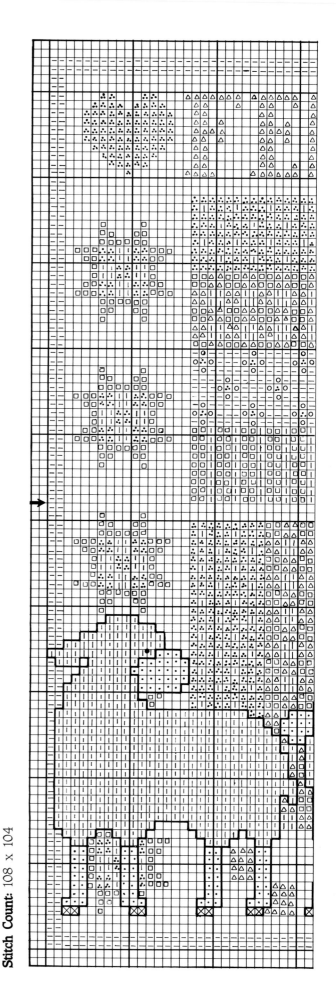

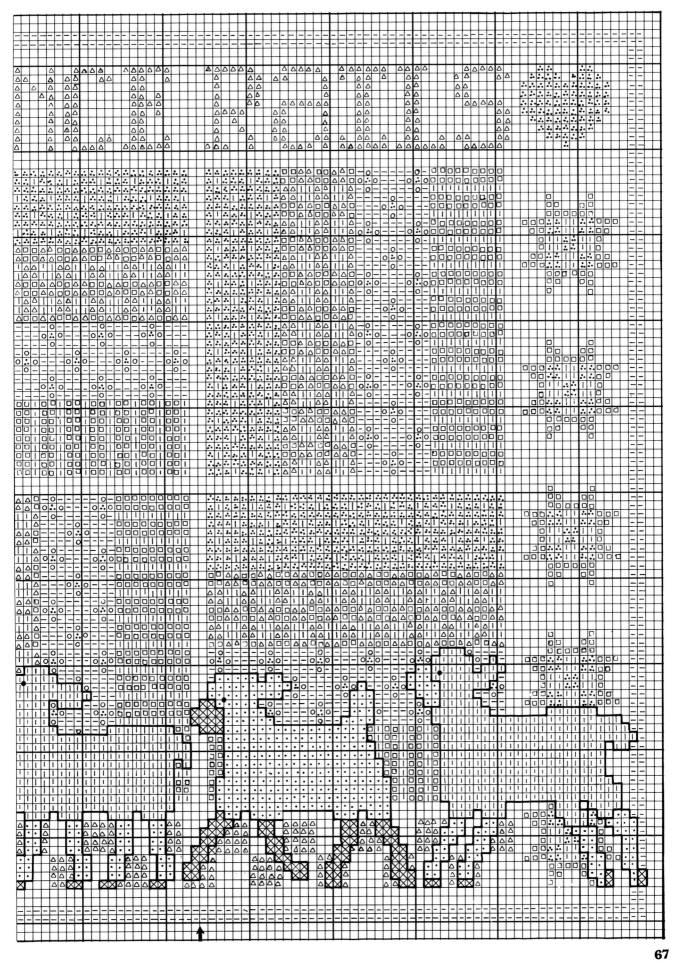

(Instructions continued from page 66.)

3. For hangers, cut a 4½" x 2½" strip from pink, blue and white fabric. With each, fold in half lengthwise and stitch. Turn and press. Loop and baste raw edges along top of design (see photo).

4. Place design on top of quilt, batting face up. Lay fabric square on top of design, right side down. Stitch through all three pieces, leaving a 4" opening to turn and keeping hangers on the inside. Turn and whipstitch opening closed. Lightly press.

5. Machine- or hand-quilt between strips.

6. Slip onto dowel to hang.

Hen and Chicks

Stitched on oatmeal rustic Aida 14, the finished design size is 7¾" x 7⅜". The fabric was cut 14" x 14".

Fabrics	Design Size
Aida 11	9⅞" x 9½"
Aida 18	6" x 5¾"
Hardanger 22	4⅞" x 4¾"

Anchor			DMC	(used for sample)
Step 1: Cross-stitch (2 strands)				
1	·			White
301	ı		744	Yellow-pale
890	–		729	Old Gold-med.
347	□		402	Mahogany-vy. lt.
349	∴		921	Copper
5968	O		355	Terra Cotta-dk.
266	△		471	Avocado Green-vy. lt.
403	●		310	Black

Step 2: Backstitch (1 strand)				
403			310	Black

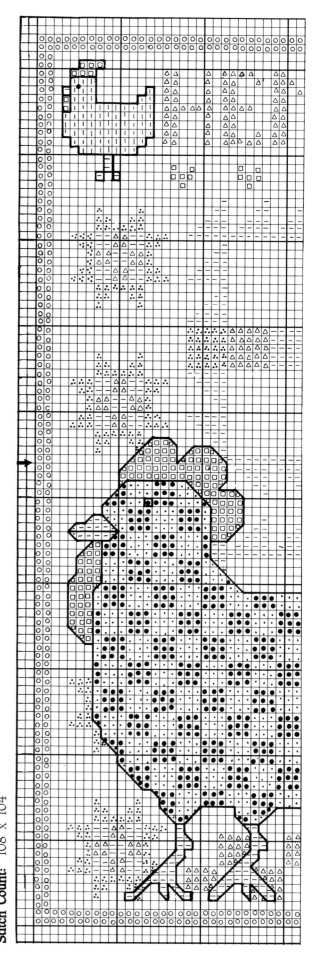

Stitch Count: 108 x 104

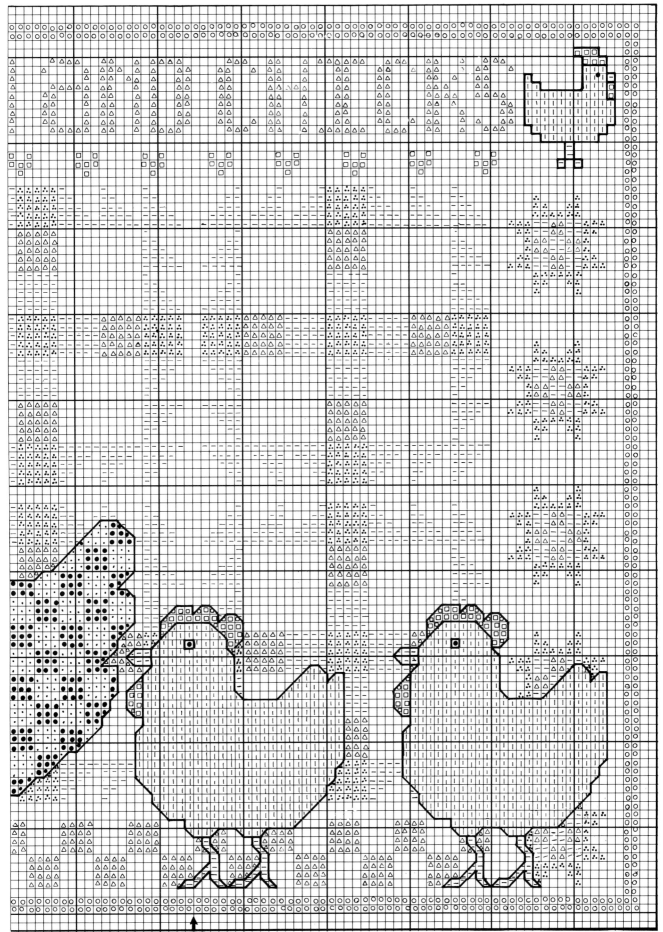

Cats in the Corner

Cats in the Corner

Stitched on wheat rustic Aida 14, the finished design size is 7¾" x 7⅜". The fabric was cut 14" x 14".

Fabrics
Fabrics	Design Size
Aida 11	9⅞" x 9½"
Aida 18	6" x 5¾"
Hardanger 22	4⅞" x 4¾"

Anchor		DMC (used for sample)	
Step 1: Cross-stitch (2 strands)			
1	·		White
886	–	677	Old Gold-vy. lt.
890	●	729	Old Gold-med.
347	△	402	Mahogany-vy. lt.
868	O	758	Terra Cotta-lt.
398	X	415	Pearl Gray
400	▲	317	Pewter Gray
403	∴	310	Black

Step 2: Backstitch (1 strand)

403	▬	310	Black

Step 3: French Knot (1 strand)

403	●	310	Black

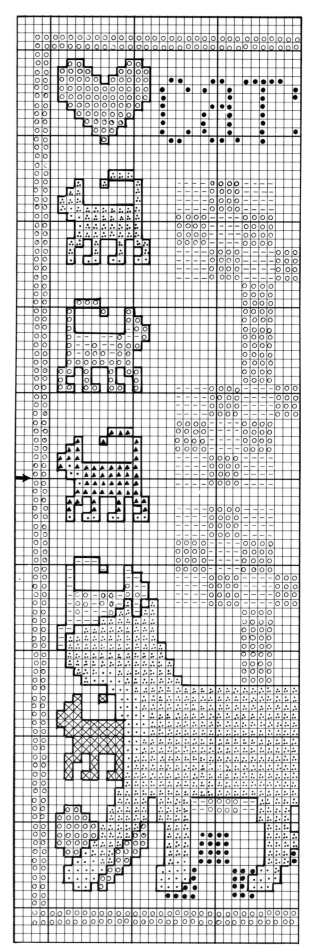

Stitch Count: 108 x 104

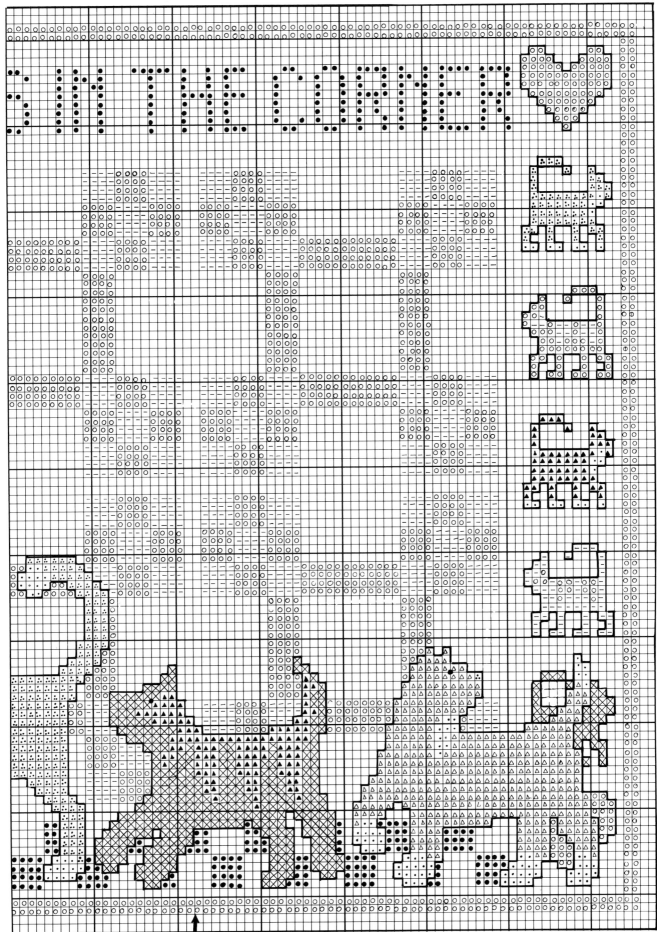

Christmas Star

Stitched on Linada 14 ct. over 1 thread, the finished design size is 7¾" x 7⅜". The fabric was
cut 14" x 14".

Fabrics
Aida 11
Aida 14
Aida 18
Hardanger 22

Design Size
9⅞" x 9½"
7¾" x 7⅜"
6" x 5¾"
4⅞" x 4¾"

Anchor		DMC (used for sample)	
Step 1: Cross-stitch (2 strands)			
1	·		White
4146	–	754	Peach-lt.
893	O	224	Shell Pink-lt.
43	X	815	Garnet-med.
858	ı	524	Fern Green-vy. lt.
244	△	987	Forest Green-dk.
309	■	435	Brown-vy. lt.
236	∴	3799	Pewter Gray-vy. dk.

Step 2: Backstitch (1 strand)

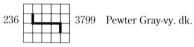

236   3799   Pewter Gray-vy. dk.

Step 3: French Knot (1 strand)

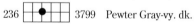

236   3799   Pewter Gray-vy. dk.

Stitch Count: 108 x 104

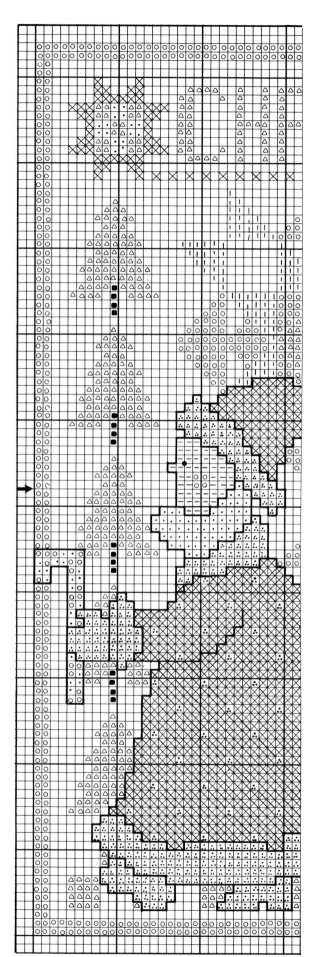

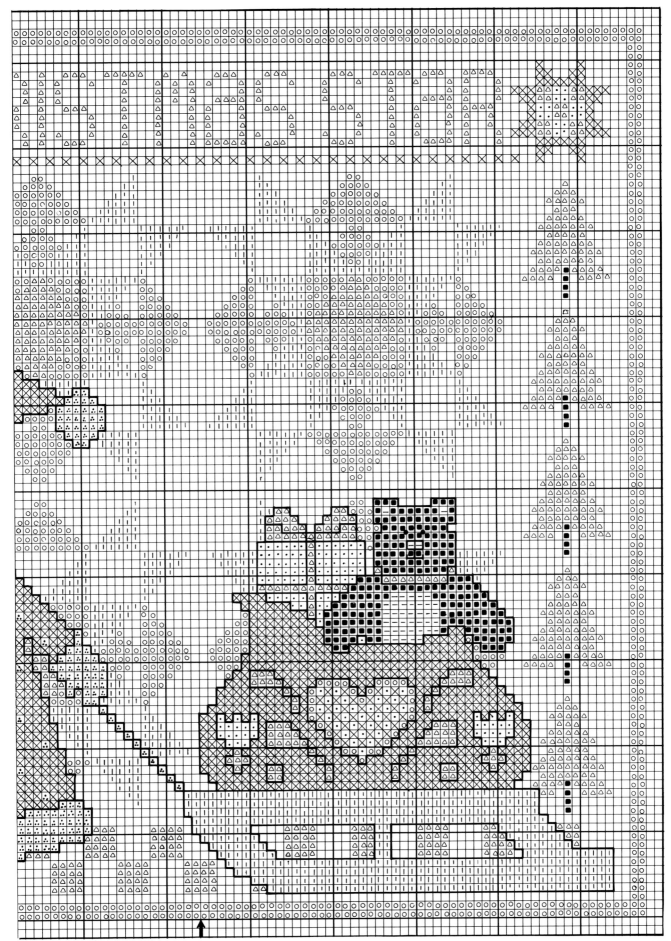

Angelic Count

Angelic Count

Angelic Count

Angelic Count

Angelic Count

Angelic Count

Angelic Count

Angelic Count

Chapter Four

Heavenly Tea

Baby's Guardian Angel

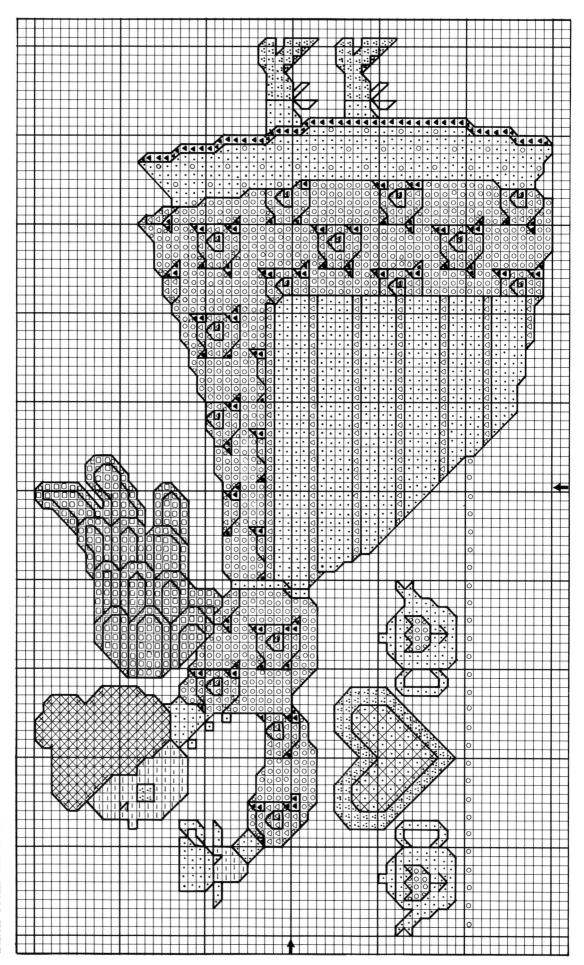

Stitch Count: 101 x 60

Heavenly Tea

Stitched on ivory Murano 30 over 2 threads, the finished design size is 6¾" x 4". The fabric was cut 13" x 10". Graph on page 80.

Fabrics	Design Size
Aida 11	9⅛" x 5½"
Aida 14	7¼" x 4¼"
Aida 18	5⅝" x 3⅜"
Hardanger 22	4⅝" x 2¾"

Anchor   **DMC (used for sample)**

Step 1: Cross-stitch (2 strands)

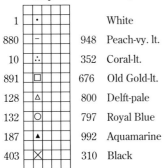

Anchor		DMC	
1	·		White
880	–	948	Peach-vy. lt.
10	∴	352	Coral-lt.
891	□	676	Old Gold-lt.
128	△	800	Delft-pale
132	○	797	Royal Blue
187	▲	992	Aquamarine
403	✕	310	Black

Step 2: Backstitch (1 strand)

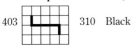

403		310	Black

Baby's Guardian Angel

Stitched on antique white Belfast linen 32 over 2 threads, the finished design size is 6½" x 4⅜". The fabric was cut 13" x 11". Graph on page 82.

Fabrics	Design Size
Aida 11	9½" x 6⅜"
Aida 14	7½" x 5"
Aida 18	5⅞" x 3⅞"
Hardanger 22	4¾" x 3⅛"

Anchor   **DMC (used for sample)**

Step 1: Cross-stitch (2 strands)

Anchor			DMC	
387	·	╱	712	Cream
366	–	╱	951	Peach Pecan-lt.
301	ı	╱	744	Yellow-pale
890	✕	╱	729	Old Gold-med.
10	△	╱	3712	Salmon-med.
50	∴	╱	3716	Wild Rose-lt.
208	○	╱	563	Jade-lt.
403	●	╱	310	Black

Step 2: Backstitch (1 strand)

403		310	Black

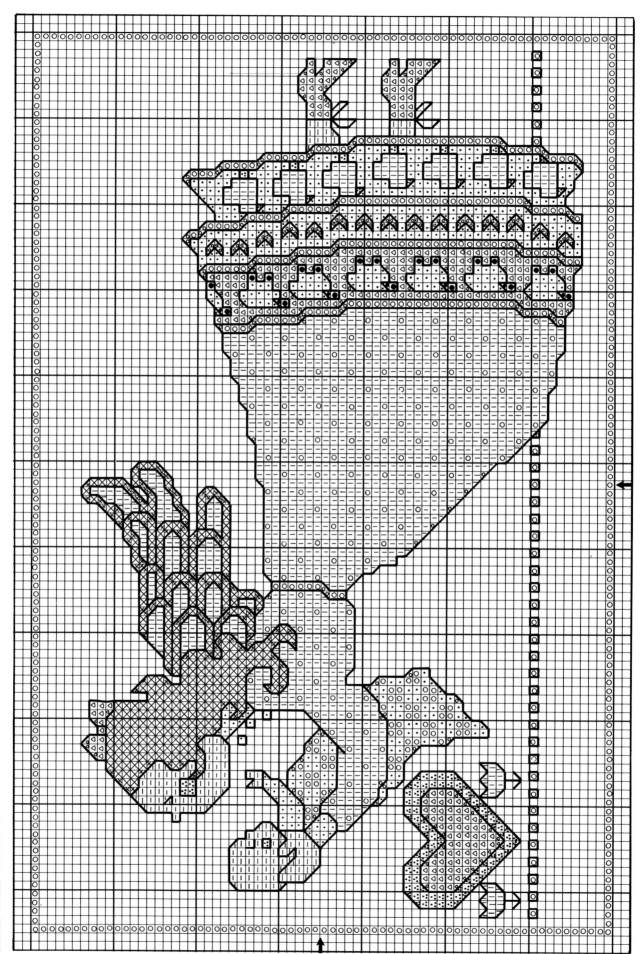

Stitch Count: 105 x 70

82

Heavenly Tea Art

For instructions, see page 115.

Baby's Guardian Angel Art

For instructions, see page 115.

Gardening Angel

Wedding Angel

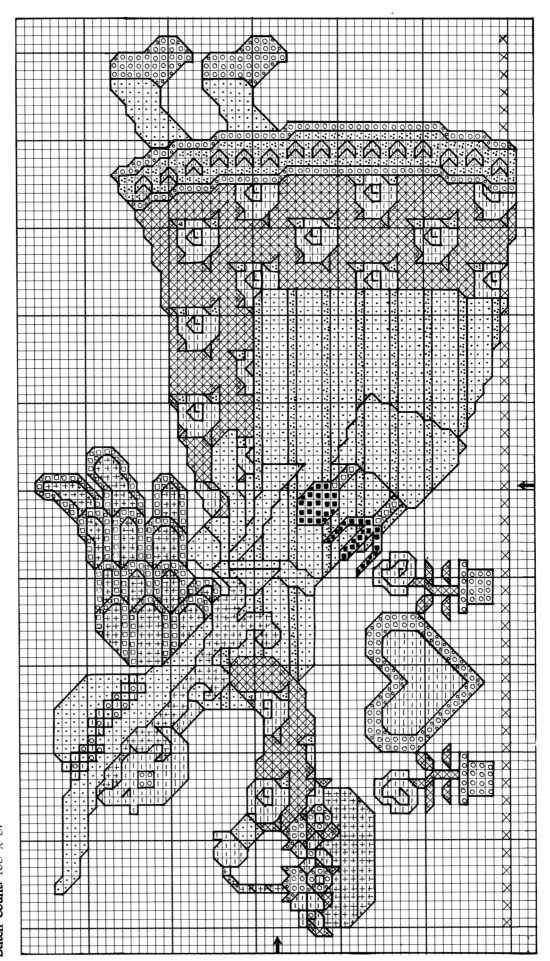

Stitch Count: 103 x 57

Gardening Angel

Stitched on mushroom Lugana 25 over 2 threads, the finished design size is 8¼" x 4½". The fabric was cut 15" x 11". Graph on page 88.

Fabrics	Design Size
Aida 11	9⅜" x 5⅛"
Aida 14	7⅜" x 4⅛"
Aida 18	5¾" x 3⅛"
Hardanger 22	4⅝" x 2⅝"

Anchor   **DMC (used for sample)**

Step 1: Cross-stitch (2 strands)

Anchor		DMC	
1	·		White
8	–	353	Peach
11	O	350	Coral-med.
203	∴	954	Nile Green
923	X	699	Christmas Green
373	+	422	Hazel Nut Brown-lt.
370	□	434	Brown-lt.
403	■	310	Black

Step 2: Backstitch (1 strand)

403	⌐	310	Black

Wedding Angel

Stitched on cream Belfast linen 32 over 2 threads, the finished design size is 6½" x 4". The fabric was cut 12" x 10". Graph on page 90.

Fabrics	Design Size
Aida 11	9½" x 5¾"
Aida 14	7½" x 4½"
Aida 18	5⅞" x 3½"
Hardanger 22	4¾" x 2⅞"

Anchor   **DMC (used for sample)**

Step 1: Cross-stitch (2 strands)

Anchor			DMC	
1	·	⁄		White
886	+	⁄	677	Old Gold-vy. lt.
890	O	⁄	729	Old Gold-med.
892	–	⁄	225	Shell Pink-vy. lt.
50	△	⁄	3716	Wild Rose-lt.
158	X	⁄	828	Blue-ultra vy. lt.
213	□	⁄	504	Blue Green-lt.

Step 2: Backstitch (1 strand)

401	⌐	413	Pewter Gray-dk.

Materials

Finished design cut to 12" x 10"
12" x 10" rectangle ivory satin fabric
1½ yards gathered off-white lace
2 yards each 4mm silk ribbon: pink, blue, lt. green
Stuffing

Directions

All seams ¼"

1. Pin lace around top edge of finished design right sides together. Stitch.

2. Lay finished design and satin fabric right sides together, making sure to tuck in lace. Stitch, leaving 3" opening. Lightly stuff and slipstitch opening closed.

3. Cut off 16" of each silk ribbon. Set aside. Using remaining ribbons, make a bow in the center of the ribbons.

4. Attach bow to upper left-hand corner of pillow. Knot ribbon tails every two inches and loosely cascade along top and side of pillow (see photo).

5. Fold remaining ribbons in half. Attach to center of bow for ring holders.

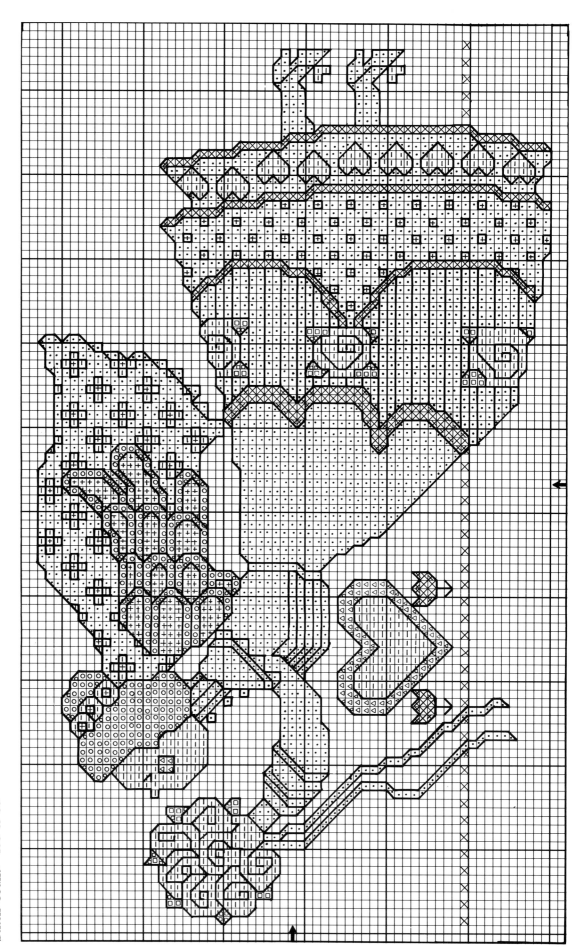

Stitch Count: 105 x 63

Wedding Angel Art

For instructions, see page 115.

Cowgirl Angel Art

For instructions, see page 115.

Native American Angel Art

For instructions, see page 115.

Cowgirl Angel

Native American Angel

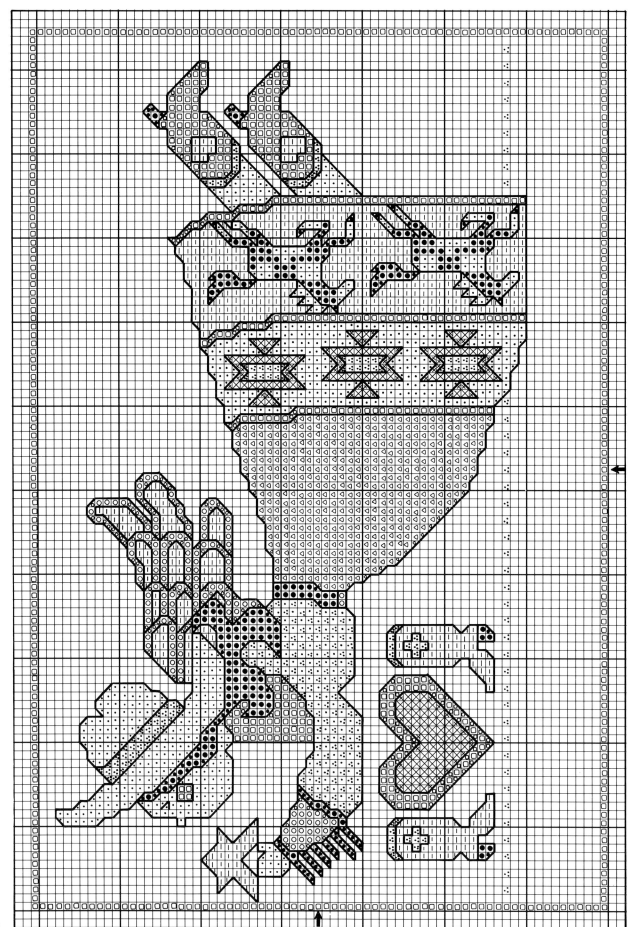

Cowgirl Angel

Stitched on light mocha Belfast linen 32 over 2 threads, the finished design size is 6½" x 4½". The fabric was cut 13" x 11". Graph on page 96.

Fabrics	Design Size
Aida 11	9½" x 6½"
Aida 14	7½" x 5⅛"
Aida 18	5⅞" x 4"
Hardanger 22	4¾" x 3¼"

Anchor		DMC (used for sample)	
Step 1: Cross-stitch (2 strands)			
933	·	543	Beige Brown-ultra vy. lt.
306	−	725	Topaz
307	⊙	783	Christmas Gold
333	☐	900	Burnt Orange-dk.
86	⊠	3608	Plum-vy. lt.
130	△	809	Delft
167	∴	597	Turquoise
403	●	310	Black
Step 2: Backstitch (1 strand)			
403		310	Black

Native American Angel

Stitched on raw Belfast linen 32 over 2 threads, the finished design size is 6¼" x 3⅝". The fabric was cut 13" x 10". Graph on page 98.

Fabrics	Design Size
Aida 11	9⅛" x 5¼"
Aida 14	7¼" x 4⅛"
Aida 18	5⅝" x 3¼"
Hardanger 22	4⅝" x 2⅝"

Anchor		DMC (used for sample)	
Step 1: Cross-stitch (2 strands)			
887	☐	3046	Yellow Beige-med.
297	⊠	743	Yellow-med.
337	·	3778	Terra Cotta
11	△	3328	Salmon-dk.
86	−	3608	Plum-vy. lt.
110	●	208	Lavender-vy. dk.
168	∴	807	Peacock Blue
403	⊙	310	Black
Step 2: Backstitch (1 strand)			
403		310	Black

Earth Angel

Stitched on cream Murano 30 over 2 threads, the finished design size is 6½" x 12¼". The fabric was cut 13" x 19".

Fabrics
Aida 11
Aida 14
Aida 18
Hardanger 22

Design Size
8⅞" x 16¾"
7" x 13⅛"
5⅛" x 10¼"
4½" x 8⅜"

Anchor		DMC	(used for sample)

Step 1: Cross-stitch (2 strands)

301	□	3822	Straw-lt.
4146	·	754	Peach-lt.
11	∴	350	Coral-med.
130	△	809	Delft
209	O	913	Nile Green-med.
355	×	975	Golden Brown-dk.
900	╱	928	Slate Green-lt.
403	–	310	Black

Step 2: Backstitch (1 strand)

403		310	Black

Step 3: French Knot (1 strand)

403	●	310	Black

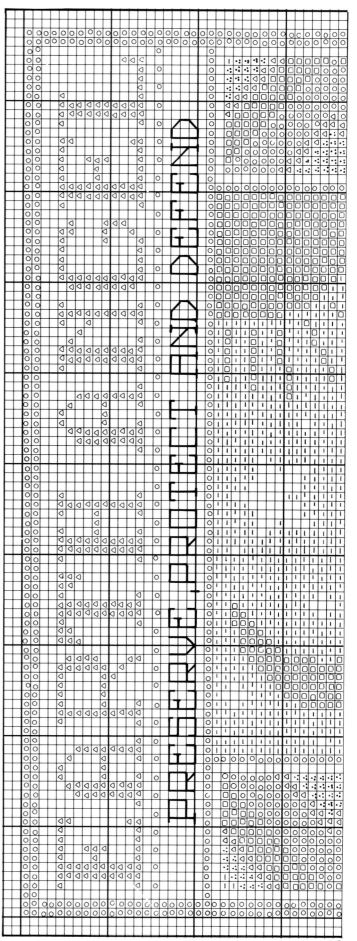

Stitch Count: 98 x 184

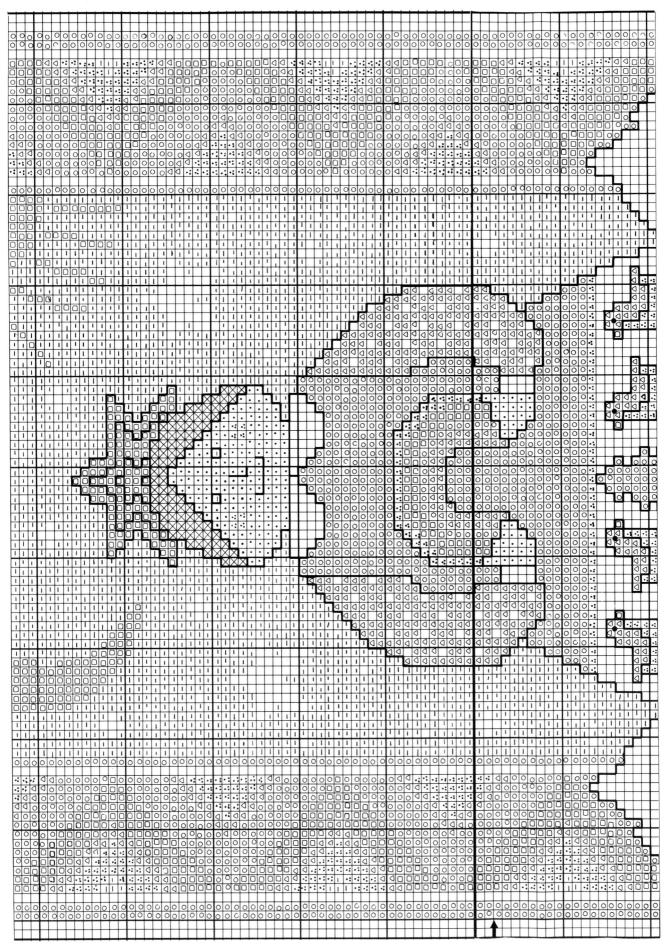

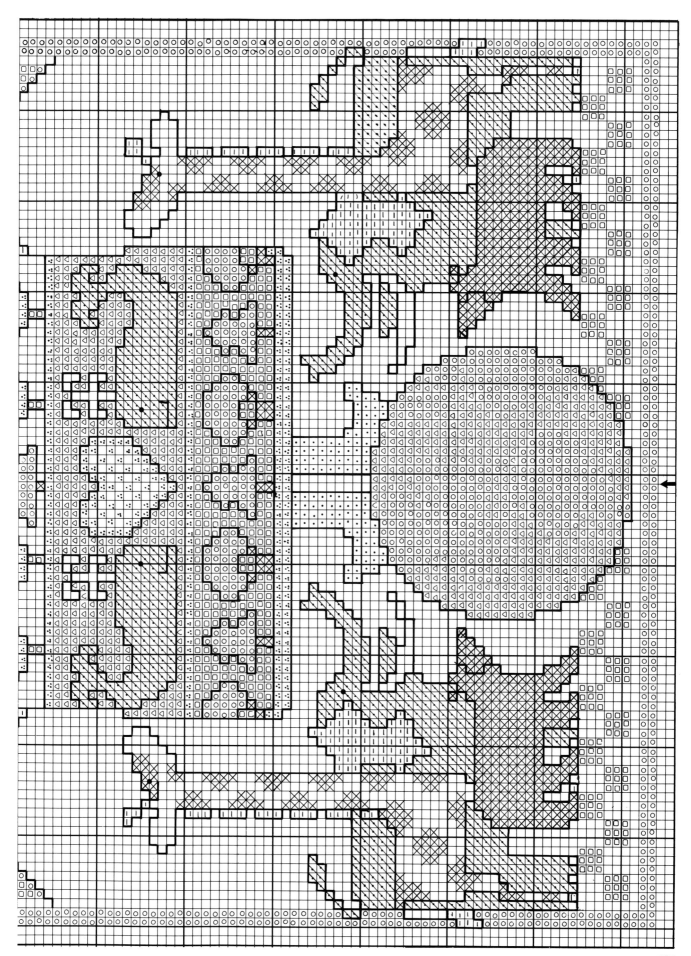

Earth Angel

Earth Angel Art

For instructions, see page 115.

Summer Celebration Angel

The HEART that loves is always YOUNG

Summer Celebration Angel Art

For instructions, see page 115.

Summer Celebration Angel

Stitched on pewter gray Murano 30 over 1 thread, the finished design size is 6¾" x 4". The fabric was cut 18" x 13".

Fabrics
Aida 11
Aida 14
Aida 18
Hardanger 22

Design Size
9⅛" x 5½"
7¼" x 4¼"
5⅝" x 3⅜"
4⅝" x 2¾"

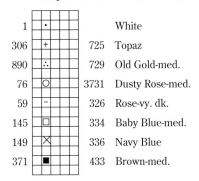

Anchor		DMC (used for sample)	

Step 1: Cross-stitch (2 strands)

1	·		White
306	+	725	Topaz
890	∴	729	Old Gold-med.
76	O	3731	Dusty Rose-med.
59	−	326	Rose-vy. dk.
145	□	334	Baby Blue-med.
149	X	336	Navy Blue
371	■	433	Brown-med.

Step 2: Backstitch (1 strand)

149		336	Navy Blue

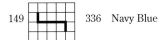

Stitch Count: 101 x 60

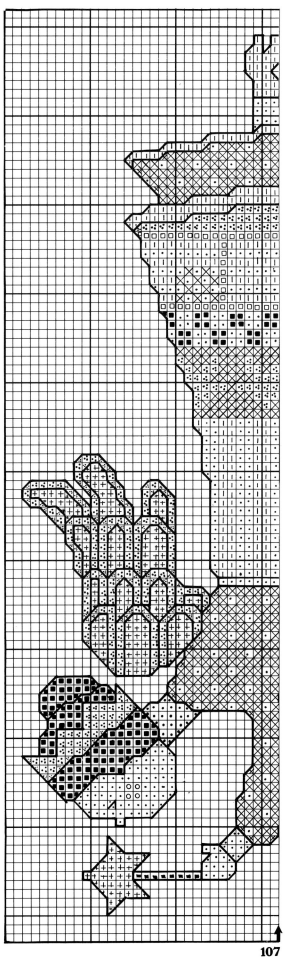

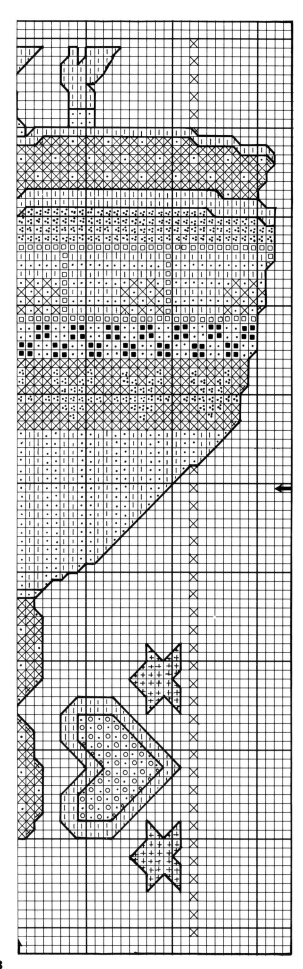

The Heart Is Always Young

Stitched on cream Belfast linen 32 over 2 threads, the finished design size is 4¼" x 6". The fabric was cut 11" x 12". Graph on page 109.

Fabrics	Design Size
Aida 11	6⅛" x 8⅞"
Aida 14	4¾" x 6⅞"
Aida 18	3¾" x 5⅜"
Hardanger 22	3" x 4⅜"

Anchor			DMC (used for sample)	
			Step 1: Cross-stitch (2 strands)	
891			676	Old Gold-lt.
880			948	Peach-vy. lt.
25			3326	Rose-lt.
118			340	Blue Violet-med.
101			550	Violet-vy. dk.
158			747	Sky Blue-vy. lt.
187			992	Aquamarine
380			839	Beige Brown-dk.

			Step 2: Backstitch (1 strand)	
101			550	Violet-vy. dk. (butterfly)
380			839	Beige Brown-dk. ((all else)

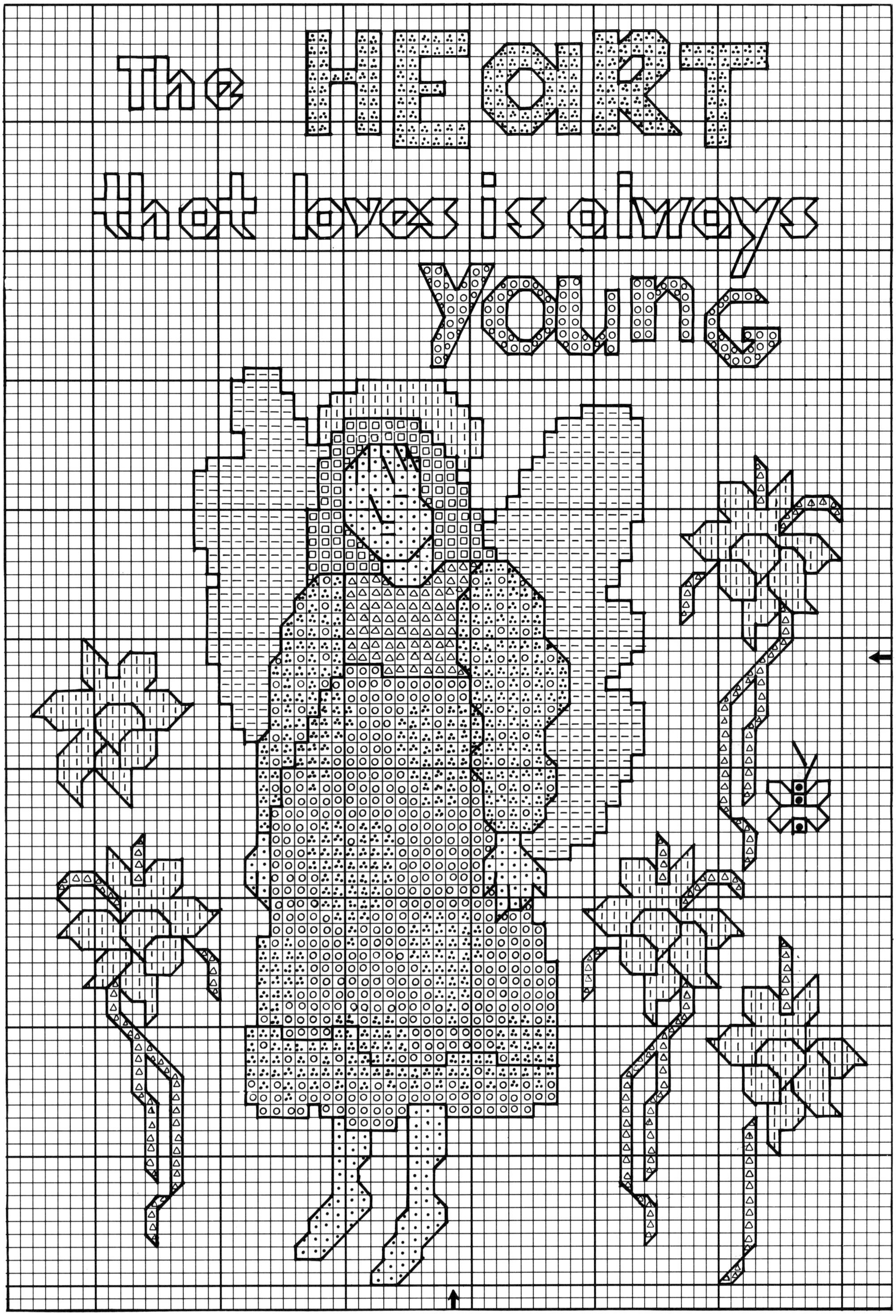
The HEART
that loves is always
young

Stitch Count: 67 x 97

Give Away Love

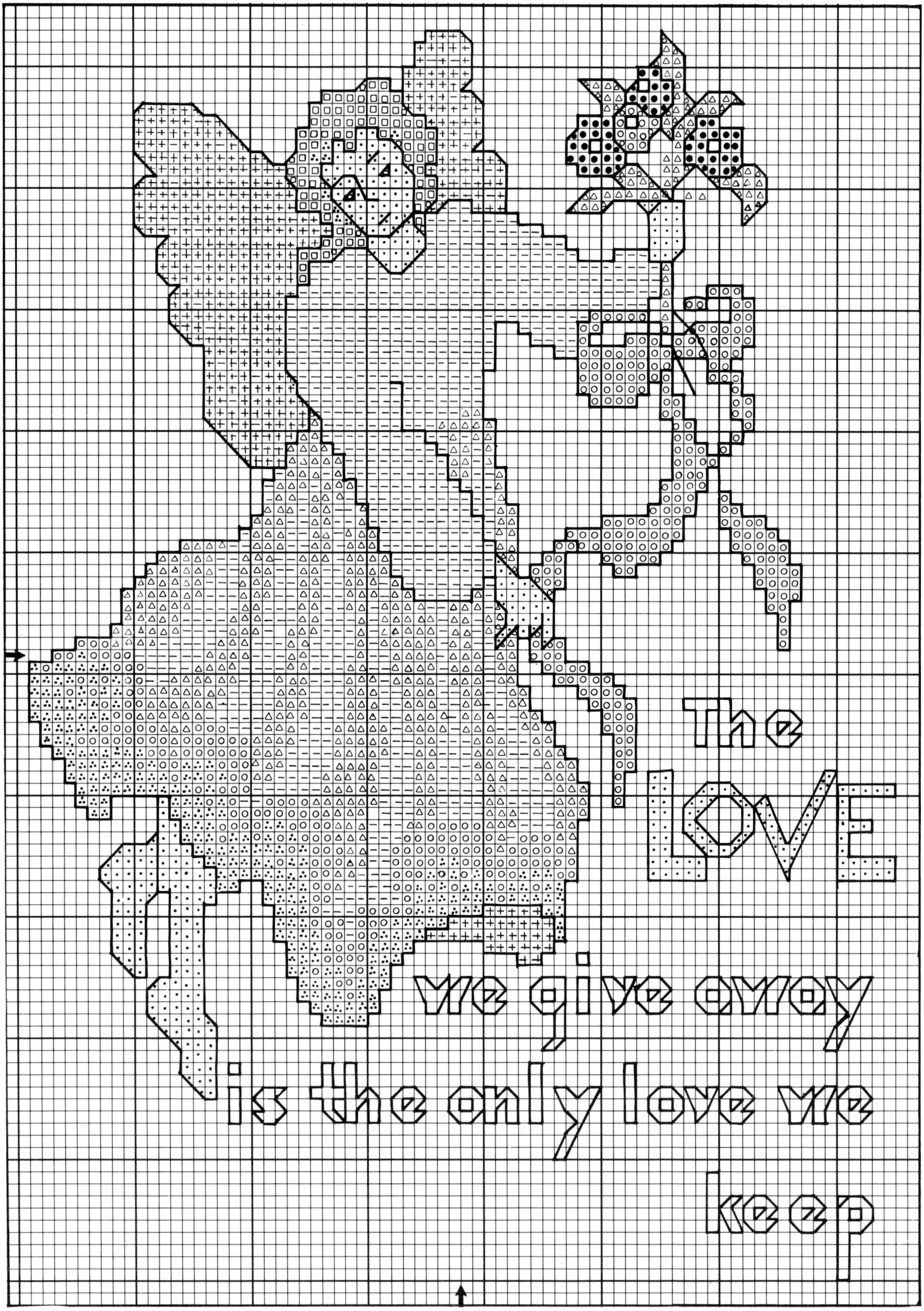
The
LOVE
we give away
is the only love we
keep

Stitch Count: 74 x 103

Give Away Love

Stitched on cream Belfast linen 32 over 2 threads, the finished design size is 4⅝" x 6½". The fabric was cut 11" x 13". Graph on page 112.

Fabrics	Design Size
Aida 11	6¾" x 9⅜"
Aida 14	5¼" x 7⅜"
Aida 18	4⅛" x 5¾"
Hardanger 22	3⅜" x 4⅜"

Anchor			DMC (used for sample)	
Step 1: Cross-stitch (2 strands)				
366	·	⁄	951	Peach Pecan-lt.
76	O	⁄	3731	Dusty Rose-med.
47	●	⁄	304	Christmas Red-med.
871	∴	⁄	3041	Antique Violet-med.
117	+	⁄	341	Blue Violet-lt.
978	–	⁄	322	Navy Blue-vy. lt.
167	△	⁄	598	Turquoise-lt.
381	□	⁄	938	Coffee Brown-ultra dk.

Step 2: Backstitch (1 strand)				
381			938	Coffee Brown-ultra dk.

Be Loveable

Stitched on cream Belfast linen 32 over 2 threads, the finished design size is 4" x 7¼". The fabric was cut 10" x 14". Graph on page 113.

Fabrics	Design Size
Aida 11	5⅜" x 10⅛"
Aida 14	4¼" x 8"
Aida 18	3¼" x 6¼"
Hardanger 22	2⅝" x 5⅛"

Anchor			DMC (used for sample)	
Step 1: Cross-stitch (2 strands)				
881	·	⁄	945	Peach Beige
891	I	⁄	676	Old Gold-lt.
8	+	⁄	761	Salmon-lt.
10	∴		3712	Salmon-med.
922	O	⁄	930	Antique Blue-dk.
158	–	⁄	747	Sky Blue-vy. lt.
875	△	⁄	503	Blue Green-med.
381	□	⁄	938	Coffee Brown-ultra dk.

Step 2: Backstitch (1 strand)				
381			938	Coffee Brown-ultra dk.

Stitch Count: 59 x 112

Fun and Easy Decoupage Frames

Follow these directions to make frames with plenty of angelic charm.

Materials

Wood frame
Color photocopy of art
Charms and bows (optional)
Acrylic paint to match finished design
Acrylic wood sealer
Liquid water-based varnish (matte or gloss)
Water
White craft glue
Brown paper sack
Dimensional fabric-and-craft pen (optional)
Lint-free cloth
Small paintbrush
Wide flat brush or sponge brush

Directions

To finish frame:
1. Sand and seal wood frame.

2. Using lint-free cloth, dust all sawdust off frame.

3. With wide flat brush or sponge, brush paint frame with acrylic paint. Two thin coats of paint work better than one thick coat.

4. Let paint completely dry. Using a piece of brown paper sack, lightly sand frame to remove any fuzz created by the acrylic paint.

To decoupage:
1. Cut out color photocopy of art.

2. Combine one-part water and one-part white craft glue. Mix well.

3. Arrange art on frame for placement.

4. Dip small paintbrush into glue-water mixture and thoroughly cover the back of the cutout piece of art.

5. Lay art onto frame. Press completely down with fingertips to squeeze out air bubbles. Smooth the excess glue with fingertips. Continue applying art until you have the look you want. *Note: If you choose to do a collage, apply the larger pieces first and follow with smaller pieces. You can let some of the pieces hang over the edges of the frame and cut them off when you are finished with the design.*

6. Let frame dry completely.

7. Using paintbrush, apply one thin coat of liquid water-base varnish. Let dry. Apply several coats for best results.

8. If desired, add charms or bows for added texture. Or you can use a dimensional fabric-and-craft pen to highlight the art.

You can purchase a pre-made decoupage mixture at a crafts or paint store if desired.

Country Holid.
Country Holid.
Country Holid.
Country Holid.
Country Holid.
Country Holid.
Country Holid.
Country Holid.

Chapter Five

Peaceable Kingdom Sampler
and Ornaments

Peaceable Kingdom Stocking

Peaceable Kingdom Sampler

Stitched on khaki Linda 27 over 2 threads, the finished design size is 7⅜" x 9⅜". The fabric was cut 14" x 17".

Fabrics	Design Size
Aida 11	9" x 11½"
Aida 14	7⅛" x 9"
Aida 18	5½" x 7"
Hardanger 22	4½" x 5¾"

Anchor			DMC	(used for sample)

Step 1: Cross-stitch (2 strands)

Anchor			DMC	Color
387	·		712	Cream
891	✕		676	Old Gold-lt.
859	–		3052	Green Gray-med.
845	△		3011	Khaki Green-dk.
879	●	◢	500	Blue Green-vy. dk.
363	□	◢	436	Tan
914	ı		3772	Pecan-med.
5975	○	◢	356	Terra Cotta-med.

Step 2: Backstitch (1 strand)

879		500	Blue Green-vy. dk.

Step 3: French Knot (1 strand)

879	●	500	Blue Green-vy. dk.

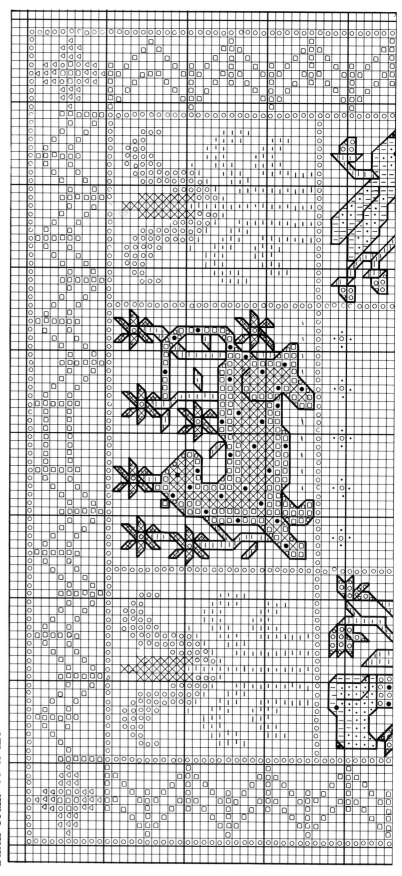

Stitch Count: 99 x 126

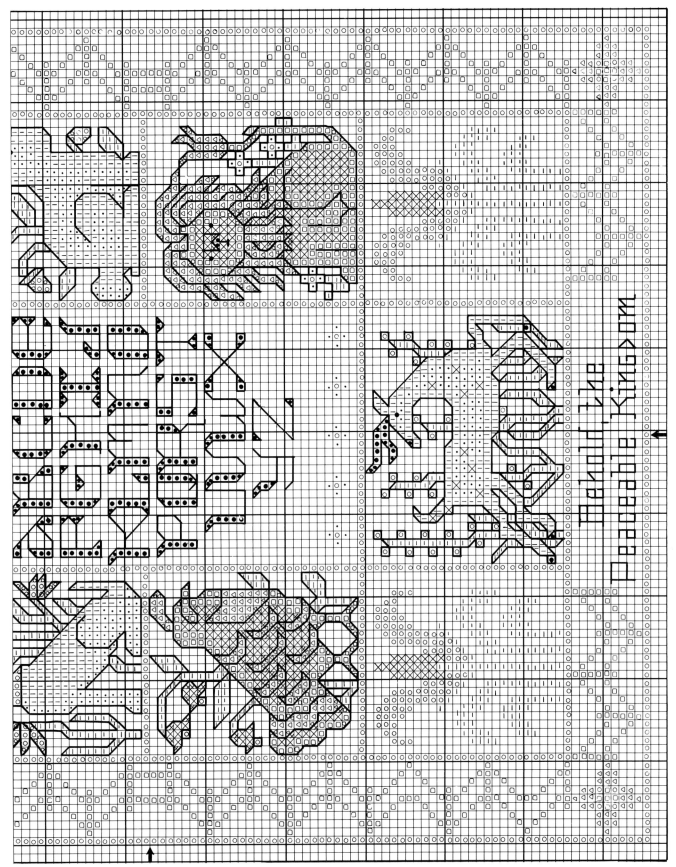

Lion   Stitch Count: 53 x 53

Rabbit   Stitch Count: 53 x 53

Quail   Stitch Count: 53 x 53

Deer   Stitch Count: 53 x 53

Dog Stitch Count: 53 x 53

Peaceable Kingdom Ornaments

Stitched on evergreen Linen 28 over 2 threads, the finished design size is 3¾" x 3¾". The fabric was cut 7" x 7".

Fabrics	Design Size
Aida 11	4¾" x 4¾"
Aida 14	3¾" x 3¾"
Aida 18	3" x 3"
Hardanger 22	2⅜" x 2⅜"

Anchor			DMC (used for sample)	

Step 1: Cross-stitch (2 strands)

Anchor			DMC	
926	△	◿		Ecru
266	+	◿	471	Avocado Green-vy. lt.
942	·	◿	738	Tan-vy. lt.
363	O	◿	436	Tan
832	∴	◿	612	Drab Brown-med.
370	☒	☒	434	Brown-lt.
352	◿	◿	300	Mahogany-vy. dk.
403	■	◿	310	Black

Step 2: Backstitch (1 strand)

403		310	Black

Step 3: French Knot (1 strand)

403	●	310	Black

Materials

Finished designs trimmed ½" around stitching
Six 3" squares of coordinating fabric
18" of narrow coordinating ribbon
Six 1" tassels

Directions

1. Trim fabric squares and finished designs to match exactly.

2. Cut ribbon into 4" lengths. Fold in half and pin to top of design. Pin tassel to bottom of design. Place fabric square on top, making sure that the ribbon and tassel are tucked inside. Sew around edges, leaving a 1" open-ing. Turn and press. Hand-stitch opening closed.

Peaceable Kingdom Stocking

Stitched on evergreen linen 28 over 2 threads, the finished design size is 9⅜" x 14¼". The fabric was cut 16" x 21".

Fabrics	Design Size
Aida 11	11⅞" x 18¼"
Aida 14	9⅜" x 14¼"
Aida 18	7¼" x 11⅛"
Hardanger 22	6" x 9⅛"

Anchor	DMC (used for sample)

Step 1: Cross-stitch (2 strands)

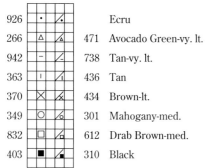

926	· /	Ecru
266	△ /	471 Avocado Green-vy. lt.
942	– /	738 Tan-vy. lt.
363	ı /	436 Tan
370	✕ /	434 Brown-lt.
349	O /	301 Mahogany-med.
832	☐ /	612 Drab Brown-med.
403	■ ▲	310 Black

Step 2: Backstitch (1 strand)

| 403 | 310 Black |

Step 3: French Knot (1 strand)

| 403 | ● | 310 Black |

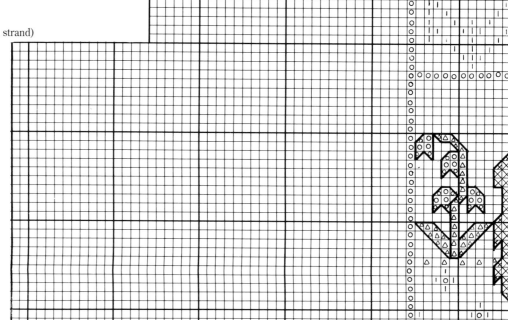

Country Holiday Cheer Stockings

(For all stockings in chapter.)

Materials

Finished design
  trimmed ½" from
  cross-stitch edge
¾ yard coordinating
  fabric
4" of cording

Directions

1. Using design as pattern cut 3 pieces from fabric. (1 for back, 2 for lining)

2. Place cross-stitch and one fabric pattern right sides together. Stack other 2 fabric patterns (lining) on top and pin in place. Turn stocking over and sew next to cross-stitch outline, leaving top open. Clip curves and turn right side out.

3. Hand-stitch lining to stocking at top opening.

4. Whipstitch cording loop at top right for hanging.

5. Add embellishments as desired.

And They Came With Haste...

And They Came With Haste...

Stitched on oatmeal Floba 25 over 2 threads, the finished design size is 15⅝" x 8½". The fabric was cut 22" x 15".

Fabrics	Design Size
Aida 11	17⅞" x 9¾"
Aida 14	14" x 7⅝"
Aida 18	10⅞" x 6"
Hardanger 22	8⅞" x 4⅞"

Anchor			DMC (used for sample)	
Step 1: Cross-stitch (2 strands)				
1	·	╱		White
9	✕	╱	760	Salmon
13	○	╱	347	Salmon-vy. dk.
147	–	╱	312	Navy Blue-lt.
210	△	╱	562	Jade-med.
942	∴	╱	738	Tan-vy. lt.
900	□	╱	3024	Brown Gray-vy. lt.
403	●	╱	310	Black
Step 2: Backstitch (1 strand)				
403			310	Black

Stitch Count: 196 x 107

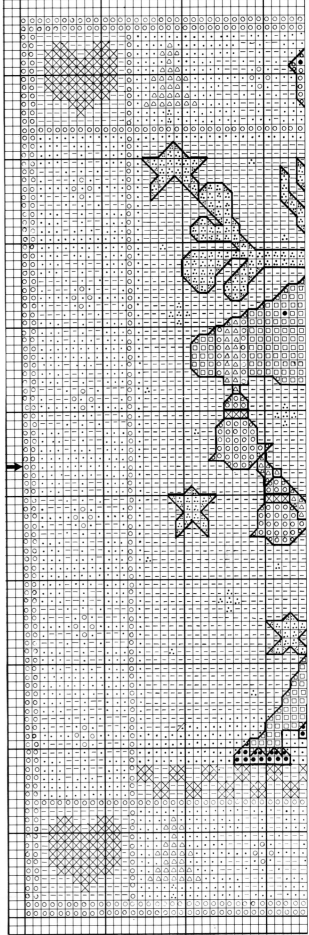

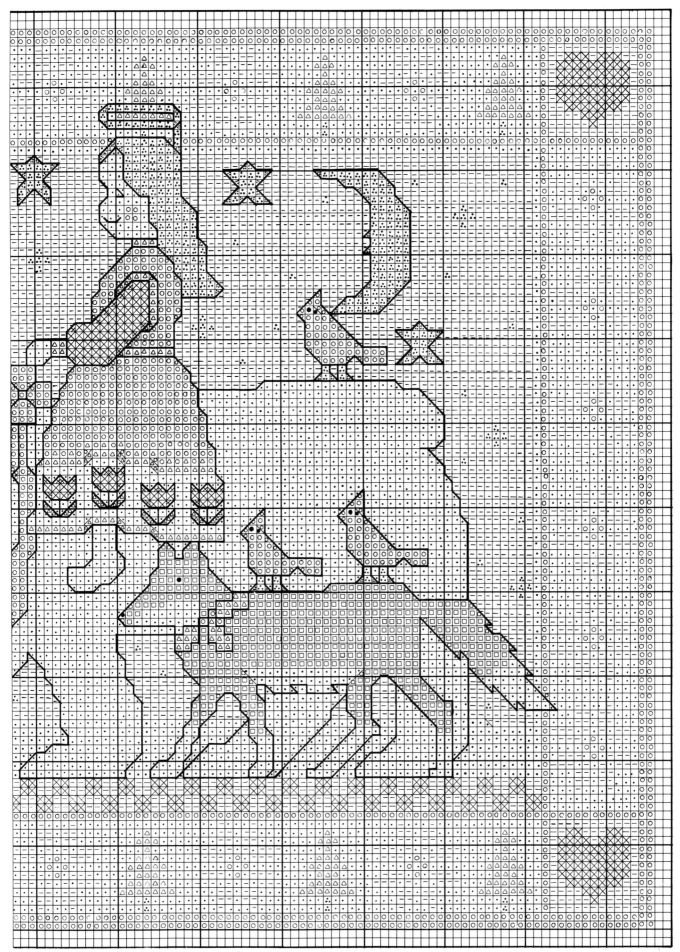

Noel Stocking

Season's Greetings

Noel Stocking

Stitch Count: 140 x 207

Stitched on pewter Murano 30 over
2 threads, the finished design size is
9⅜" x 13¾" The fabric was cut 16"
x 20".

Fabrics | Design Size

Fabrics	Design Size
Aida 11	12¾" x 18⅞"
Aida 14	10" x 14¾"
Aida 18	7¾" x 11½"
Hardanger 22	6⅜" x 9⅜"

Anchor		DMC	(used for sample)

Step 1: Cross-stitch (2 strands)

1	·		White
890	∴ /	729	Old Gold-med.
50	△	605	Cranberry-vy. lt.
78	○	601	Cranberry-dk.
168	✕	807	Peacock Blue
186	−	993	Aquamarine-lt.
189	▲	991	Aquamarine-dk.
403	●	310	Black

Step 2: Backstitch (1 strand)

| 403 | | 310 | Black |

Step 3: French Knot (1 strand)

| 403 | ● | 310 | Black |

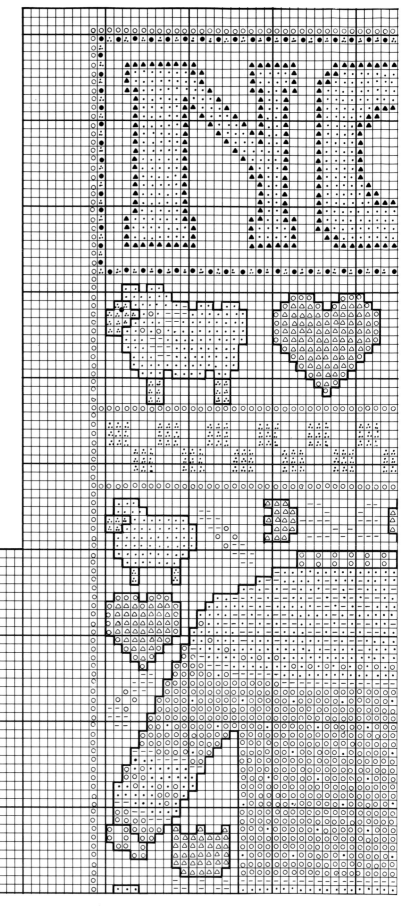

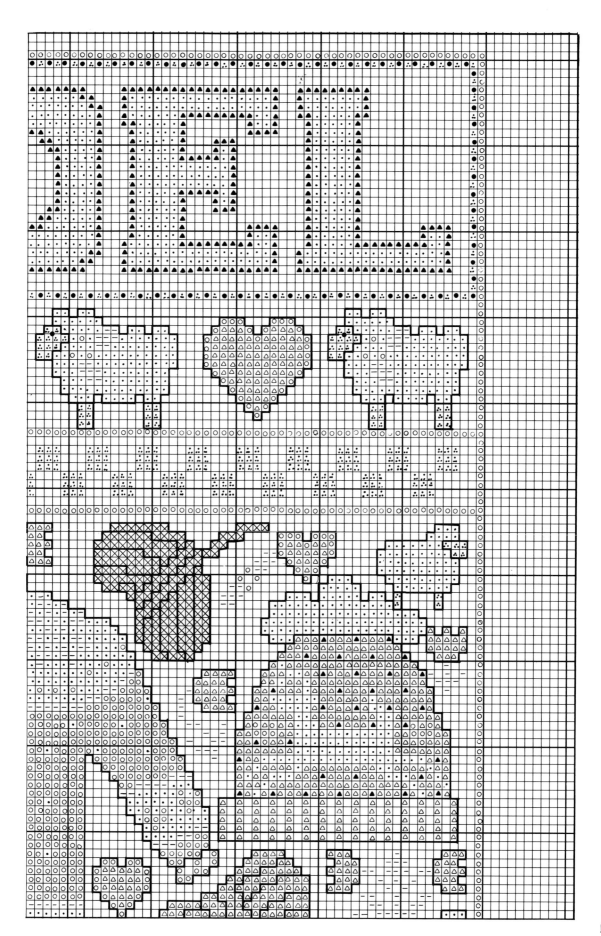

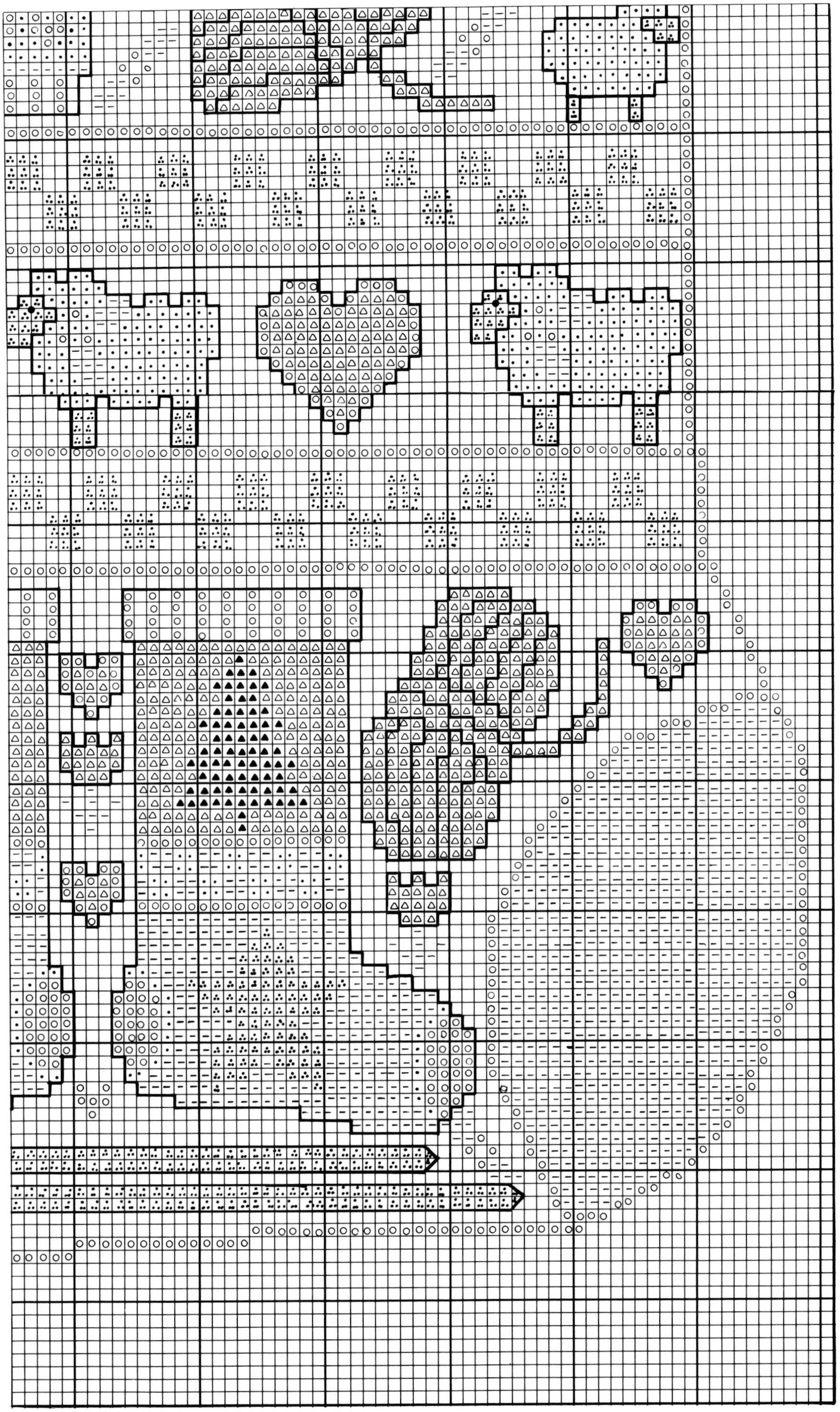

Season's Greetings

Stitched on oatmeal Floba 25 over 2 threads, the finished design size is 16¼" x 10⅝" The fabric was cut 23" x 17".

Fabrics	Design Size
Aida 11	18½" x 12⅛"
Aida 14	14½" x 9½"
Aida 18	11¼" x 7⅜"
Hardanger 22	9¼" x 6"

Anchor		DMC (used for sample)	
Step 1: Cross-stitch (2 strands)			
301	·	744	Yellow-pale
4146	−	754	Peach-lt.
11	O	350	Coral-med.
160	ı	813	Blue-lt.
258	△	905	Parrot Green-dk.
309	□	435	Brown-vy. lt.
382	∴	3021	Brown Gray-vy. dk.
403	✕	310	Black
Step 2: Backstitch (1 strand)			
403	⌐	310	Black
Step 3: French Knot (1 strand)			
403	●	310	Black

Stitch Count: 203 x 133

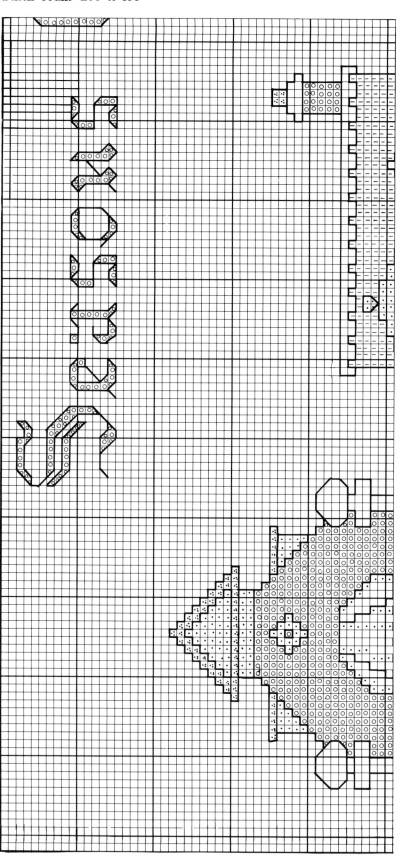

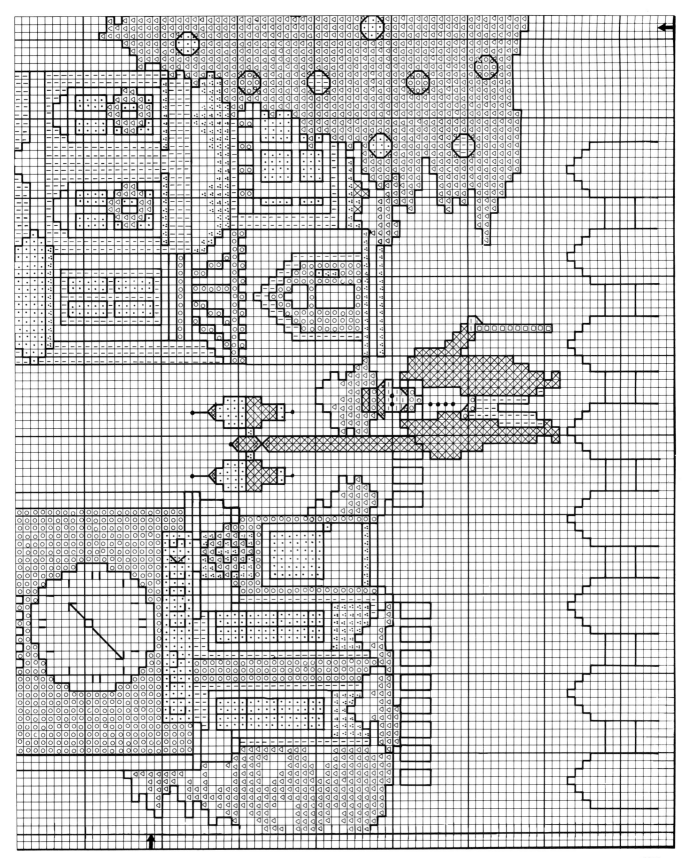

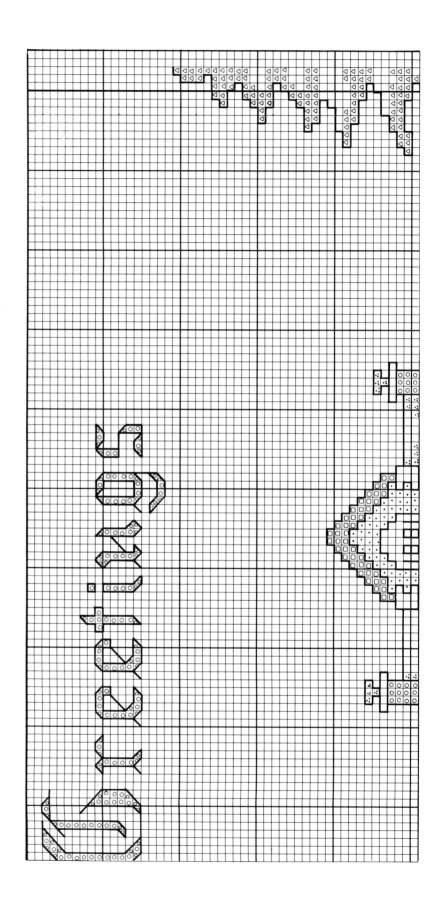

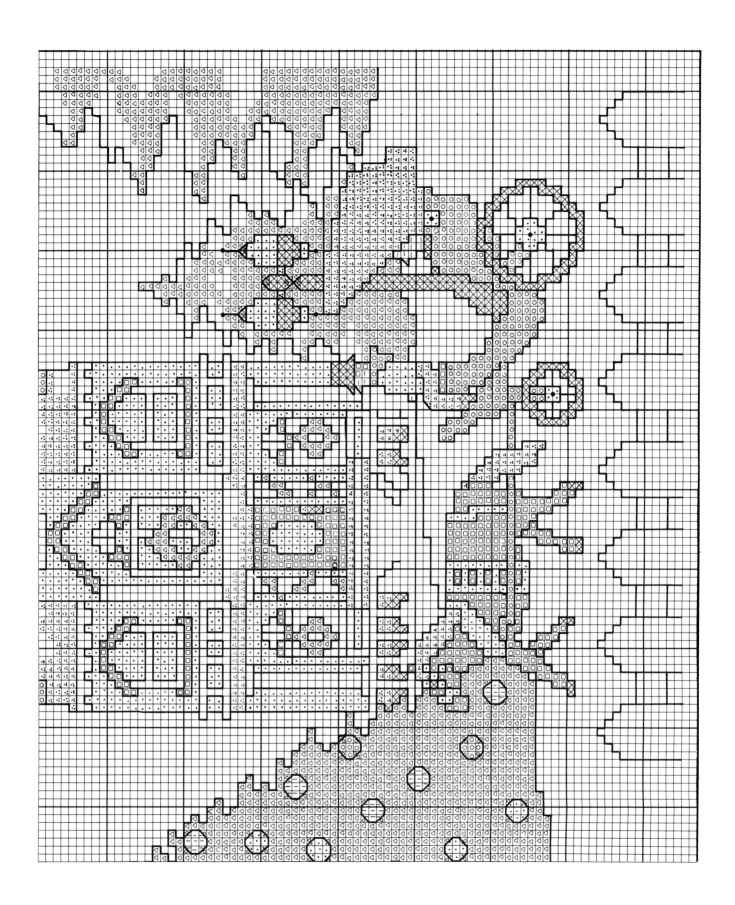

General Instructions

Cross-stitch: Make one cross-stitch for each symbol on chart. Bring needle up at A, down at B, up at C, down at D; see Diagram 1. For rows, stitch across fabric from left to right to make half-crosses and then back to complete stitches; see Diagram 2.

Diagram 1

Diagram 2

French Knot: Bring the needle up at A, using one strand of embroidery floss. Wrap floss around needle two times (unless indicated otherwise in instructions). Insert needle beside A, pulling floss until it fits snugly around needle. Pull needle through to back.

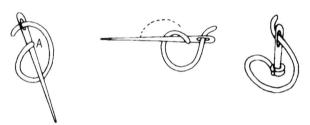

Fabrics: Designs in this book are worked on even-weave fabrics made especially for cross-stitch, which can be found in most needlework shops. Fabrics used for models are identified in sample information by color, name, and thread count per inch.

Preparing fabric: Cut fabric at least 3" larger on all sides than finished design size or cut as indicated in sample information to ensure enough space for project assembly. To keep fabric from fraying, whipstitch or machine-zigzag along raw edges or apply liquid ravel preventer.

Needles: Choose needle that will slip easily through fabric holes without piercing fabric threads. For fabric with 11 or fewer threads per inch, use needle size 24; for 14 threads per inch, use needle size 24 or 26; for 18 or more threads per inch, use needle size 26. Never leave needle in design area of fabric. It may leave rust or permanent impression on fabric.

Finished design size: To determine size of finished design, divide stitch count by number of threads per inch of fabric. When design is stitched over two threads, divide stitch count by half the threads per inch.

Floss: Use 18" lengths of floss. For best coverage, separate strands. Dampen with wet sponge. Then put back together number of strands called for in color code.

Stitching method: For smooth stitches, use push-and-pull method. Starting on wrong side of fabric, bring needle straight up, pulling floss completely through to right side. Reinsert needle and bring it back straight down, pulling needle and floss completely through to back of fabric. Keep floss flat, but do not pull thread tight. For even stitches, tension should be consistent throughout.

Sewing Hints:

Slipstitch: With a needle and thread, make small, almost invisible stitches. Slipstitching is used to secure a folded edge to a flat surface.

Whipstitch: A whipstitch is usually used to join two finished edges, but it can also be used to secure an edge to a background fabric. Using a single strand of thread (unless otherwise indicated) knotted at one end, insert needle at 1 and pick up a few threads of both layers of fabric, bringing it out at 2.

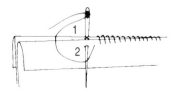

Metric Equivalency Chart

MM-Millimetres   CM-Centimetres

INCHES TO MILLIMETRES AND CENTIMETRES

INCHES	MM	CM	INCHES	CM	INCHES	CM
⅛	3	0.3	9	22.9	30	76.2
¼	6	0.6	10	25.4	31	78.7
½	13	1.3	12	30.5	33	83.8
⅝	16	1.6	13	33.0	34	86.4
¾	19	1.9	14	35.6	35	88.9
⅞	22	2.2	15	38.1	36	91.4
1	25	2.5	16	40.6	37	94.0
1¼	32	3.2	17	43.2	38	96.5
1½	38	3.8	18	45.7	39	99.1
1¾	44	4.4	19	48.3	40	101.6
2	51	5.1	20	50.8	41	104.1
2½	64	6.4	21	53.3	42	106.7
3	76	7.6	22	55.9	43	109.2
3½	89	8.9	23	58.4	44	111.8
4	102	10.2	24	61.0	45	114.3
4½	114	11.4	25	63.5	46	116.8
5	127	12.7	26	66.0	47	119.4
6	152	15.2	27	68.6	48	121.9
7	178	17.8	28	71.1	49	124.5
8	203	20.3	29	73.7	50	127.0

YARDS TO METRES

YARDS	METRES	YARDS	METRES	YARDS	METRES	YARDS	METRES	YARDS	METRES
⅛	0.11	2⅛	1.94	4⅛	3.77	6⅛	5.60	8⅛	7.43
¼	0.23	2¼	2.06	4¼	3.89	6¼	5.72	8¼	7.54
⅜	0.34	2⅜	2.17	4⅜	4.00	6⅜	5.83	8⅜	7.66
½	0.46	2½	2.29	4½	4.11	6½	5.94	8½	7.77
⅝	0.57	2⅝	2.40	4⅝	4.23	6⅝	6.06	8⅝	7.89
¾	0.69	2¾	2.51	4¾	4.34	6¾	6.17	8¾	8.00
⅞	0.80	2⅞	2.63	4⅞	4.46	6⅞	6.29	8⅞	8.12
1	0.91	3	2.74	5	4.57	7	6.40	9	8.23
1⅛	1.03	3⅛	2.86	5⅛	4.69	7⅛	6.52	9⅛	8.34
1¼	1.14	3¼	2.97	5¼	4.80	7¼	6.63	9¼	8.46
1⅜	1.26	3⅜	3.09	5⅜	4.91	7⅜	6.74	9⅜	8.57
1½	1.37	3½	3.20	5½	5.03	7½	6.86	9½	8.69
1⅝	1.49	3⅝	3.31	5⅝	5.14	7⅝	6.97	9⅝	8.80
1¾	1.60	3¾	3.43	5¾	5.26	7¾	7.09	9¾	8.92
1⅞	1.71	3⅞	3.54	5⅞	5.37	7⅞	7.20	9⅞	9.03
2	1.83	4	3.66	6	5.49	8	7.32	10	9.14

Index

American Antiques — 11
    code — 12
    graph — 12–13
    alphabet — 29

And They Came With Haste... — 128
    code — 129
    graph — 129–131

Angler's Rest — 17
    code — 20
    graph — 20–21
    alphabet — 30

Antique Thread Spool — 49

Baby's Guardian Angel — 79

    code — 81
    graph — 82
    art — 84

Be Lovable — 111
    code — 113
    graph — 114

Index

Bunnies in a Basket 38
    code 42
    graph 40-41
    finishing 42

"C" Is for Cat 39
    code 42
    graph 43

Cats in the Corner 70
    code 72
    graph 72-73

Christmas Sleigh 23
    code 26
    graph 27-28
    alphabet 31

Christmas Star 71
    code 74
    graph 74-75

Come On In 35
    code 36
    graph 37

Country Farm 58
    code 60
    graph 60-61

Country Garden 22
    code 26
    graph 27-28
    alphabet 31

Country Holiday Cheer Stockings 126

Country Home 10
    code 12
    graph 12-13
    alphabet 29

Country Welcome Banners 19

Cowgirl Angel 94
    code 97
    graph 96
    art 92

Cross-stitch 142

Decoupage frames 115

Earth Angel 102
    code 99
    graph 99-101
    art 103

Espresso Yourself 44
    code 48
    graph 46-47

Fabric 142

Farm Fresh 50
    code 53
    graph 53

Fence Rails 64
    code 66
    graph 66-67
    finishing 66,68

Finished design 142

Floss 142

French knot 142

Gardening Angel 86
    code 89
    graph 88
    art 85

Give Away Love 110
    code 112
    graph 113

Goose Waddle 59
    code 62
    graph 62-63

Heart Is Always Young, The 105
    code 107
    graph 108

Heavenly Tea 78
    code 81
    graph 80
    art 83

Hen and Chicks 65
    code 68
    graph 68-69

Home Sweet Home 34
    code 36
    graph 36

Hunter's Rest 16
    code 19
    graph 18
    alphabet 30

Native American Angel 95
    code 97
    graph 96
    art 93

Needles 142

Noel Stocking 132
    code 134

graph 134-137

Peaceable Kingdom Ornaments 118
    code 122-123
    graph 123
    finishing 123

Peaceable Kingdom Sampler 118
    code 120
    graph 120-121

Peaceable Kingdom Stocking 119
    code 124
    graph 124-127
    finishing 126

Preparing fabric 142

Season's Greetings 133
    code 138
    graph 138-141

Sewing hints 142

Slipstitch 142

Stitching method 142

Summer Celebration Angel 104
    code 107
    graph 106
    alphabet 109

Sunshine House 51
    code 53
    graph 54-55

Three Coffee Cups 45
    code 48
    graph 46-47
    finishing 49

Wedding Angel 87
    code 89
    graph 90
    finishing 89
    art 91

Whipstitch 142

Eight-Color Coun

Eight-Color Coun

Eight-Color Coun

Eight-Color Coun

Eight-Color Coun

Eight-Color Coun

Eight-Color Coun

Eight-Color Coun